The Big Book of
20 AWESOME
Paper Planes

Table of Contents

Levels: ○ 1-Easy   ○ 2-Intermediate   ○ 3-Difficult

Why Do We Fly Paper Planes?

A paper plane represents freedom. To soar above the earth, floating on a current of air like a bird in flight, is a hope that lives inside us all. Since ancient times, man has dreamt of imitating the beating wings of a bird. We have made great advances in powered flight, yet the paper plane a simple, wing-shaped, human-powered toy still embodies the age-old desire to fly. This book presents paper plane designs from around the globe, ranging from easy gliders for the beginner to challenging flights of fancy for the experienced aero-engineer. Once you have mastered the basics, you might want to try designing your own planes, or creating games and competitions. The sky is the limit!

Don't worry. To be a master, you will make plenty of these.

Get ready to fold your way to being a master paper plane flyer.

GOOD LUCK!

Off to a Flying Start

Paper and Folding Instructions

Each awesome paper plane in this book requires only a single sheet of 8-1/2" X 11" (21.5 cm X 28 cm) paper. No cutting, taping, or gluing needed. Test each design with a plain sheet of paper, before using the printed sheets provided in the back of the book. This way, if you make a mistake, it's not with the good stuff.

Keep the paper flat or in the paper sleeve until you're ready to use it. Always start with Side 1 up (see diagram below). To see which side is side one, check the paper symbol located at the top of each page. Match the paper design to the correct plane design.

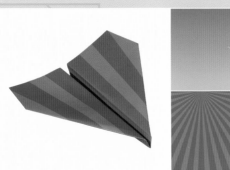

Side 1

Side 2

Note: Keep the paper away from humid or damp air. Don't use any sheets that have bent corners or buckle marks. These flaws could disturb the airflow over the paper's surface.

Types of Paper

Once you have used all the paper provided, try experimenting with different papers. Avoid using paper that is too heavy (construction paper, watercolor paper, drawing paper) or too light (tissue paper, paper towels, tissue). Photocopy paper is the ideal weight and thickness and comes in different shades. Unusual papers you might want to consider include patterned wrapping paper, junk mail, paper-backed metallic, quality color magazine paper, disposable table cloths, thin tracing paper, and lightweight homemade paper.

For the best flying results, make sure the right side and the left side mirror each other when folding. The slightest mistake can make a big difference.

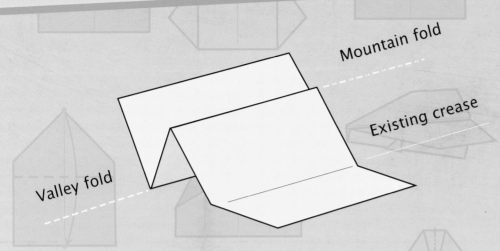

Mountain fold

Existing crease

Valley fold

How to Fold

Always fold on a hard surface, such as a tabletop or a large hardback book, and make sharp creases—never fold entirely in the air, on your lap, or using a soft surface, such as a carpet. The first drawing of each plane shows an existing crease, or creases, that divide the paper in half or quarters. Fold neatly and accurately, making sure that edges or corners meet exactly as indicated. Smooth the layers flat after each step.

Symbols

The symbols in this book are commonly used in paper plane books throughout the world. The most important thing to understand is the difference between a Mountain fold and a Valley fold. Each step builds on the other, so keep looking ahead to see the results of what you are doing now. Refer to this guide whenever you run into an unfamiliar symbol.

Valley fold

- - - - - - - - - -

Mountain fold

— · — · — · —

Existing crease

————————

X-ray view

· · · · · · · · · · · ·

Turn the paper over

Fold forward

Fold behind (back)

Fold dot to dot

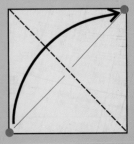

Crease, then unfold

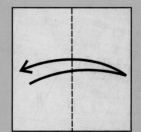

Flying Tips

Tweaking

Experiencing a failure to launch? First off, think of the first throw as a test to see how well the plane performs. Does it nosedive, stall, dive-bomb, or barrel-roll? Once you've identified the problem, you can try to solve it. However, keep in mind that planes are fickle. A plane that dives for one person may stall when somebody else throws it, or a glider that sails majestically into the distance on the first throw may never do it again. There are some reliable ways to improve performance, usually involving the perfect combination of trimming and launching. Adjusting the angle the wings make across the top of the fuselage is a good place to start. Checking the symmetry, elevators (which make the plane go up and down), and ailerons (which make the plane bank or roll) are other tweaking methods.

Safety Tip:
Never throw a plane directly at another person, especially if the plane has a sharp, pointed nose.

Speed

Novice plane fliers tend to throw a paper plane either too softly, so it never catches the air and wafts drowsily to the ground, or with so much force it barrels rapidly through the air before meeting a violent end. Most planes do best with moderate force, although experimenting with different speeds can yield successful results.

Throwing angles

The four main angles of launch are vertically upward, diagonally upward, horizontal, and downward. Vertically upward requires speed and athleticism, as the intention is to hurl the plane as high as possible before it starts to level out and begin its stately descent. Diagonally upward at an angle between 30 degrees and 45 degrees is the most familiar and versatile launch, especially at moderate speeds. Play around with the precise angle of launch—too steep can make the plane stall, too shallow can reduce the distance or length of the flight. Horizontal launching results in steady, unassuming flights and is best for delicate gliders in limited spaces. Downward launching may seem like a kamikaze mission, but it can create spectacular acrobatic flights. Always throw downward launches with great speed, and never gently.

Indoors/Outdoors

Darts and slow gliders are ideal for the indoor's calm air and confined space. Outdoors, hardier, heavier planes make the best fliers, but small darts and high-flying gliders are also ace performers.

Flying Guide

Darts

These planes are built for distance and speed. They are sleek and streamlined, not a wasted angle. Throw dart planes straight or at an upward, 45-degree angle, and launch it like you mean it. A hard throw is the best throw.

Remember! If the plane has narrow wings throw the plane harder. If the plane has wide wings throw the plane softer.

Not all Dart planes will have the pointed nose tip.

Darts fly best when thrown within this angle range

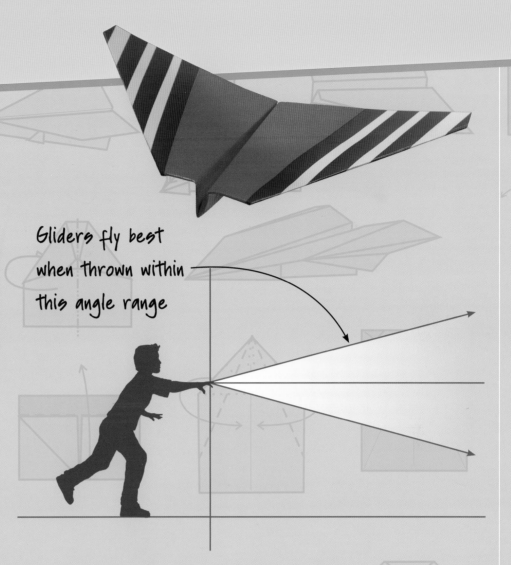

Gliders

The name says it all: gliders drift on streams of air. They fly long and slow, making wide, lazy turns and rarely land without gently bumping into something first. Most gliders are room-crossers, and can be launched with a smooth, even motion—remember, you are guiding the plane, not throwing it. On the other hand, high flier gliders are launched like a rocket—straight up, as if trying to poke a hole in the moon.

Gliders fly best when thrown within this angle range

Stunt planes fly best when thrown within these angle ranges

Stunt

Stunt planes are the barnstormers of the paper plane world and the hardest working aircraft in the business—looping, circling, diving, and rolling and then coming back for more! Stunt planes can be thrown all sorts of ways, but the best method is with a medium-strength throw that is up and away from your body.

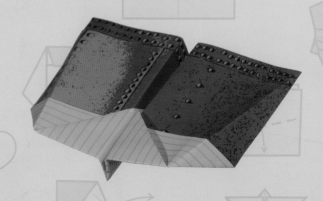

History of Paper Planes

Paper planes are a form of aerogami, a variation on origami, the Japanese art of paper folding. Although no one has pinpointed exactly when the first tiny glider sailed through the air, using paper to create toys has been around for at least 2,000 years, when kites were a popular form of entertainment in China. In the late 1700s, the Montgolfier brothers of France invented the hot air balloon. Their earliest models were made partly of paper. The inventor of model gliders is said to have been George Cayley, an English squire. He built hand-launched, kite-like gliders from linen in the early 1800s.

The Wright Brothers, two Americans credited with building the first successful airplane, may have experimented with paper models, but the earliest known date of using paper planes to test aerodynamics can be found in aviation magazine articles dating back to 1909. Two decades later, Jack Northrup, cofounder of the Lockheed Corporation, widely used paper planes to try out ideas for flying real-life aircraft.

PAPER PLANES RULE!

In 1944, model paper plane designs were offered by General Mills Corporation for two Wheaties® cereal box tops and the princely sum of five cents. Since WWII, paper planes have introduced millions of kids and adults to the pleasures of building models and flying their creations.

Are you ready to make paper planes?

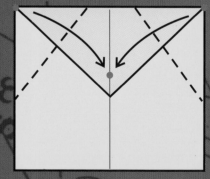

◀ - - - - - - - - Remember...this is Side One.

Eastern Star

A stellar model that glides perfectly. This glider requires a gentle throw that starts by holding the plane midway under the wings.

1

Side One

Fold and unfold to create a vertical middle crease.

2

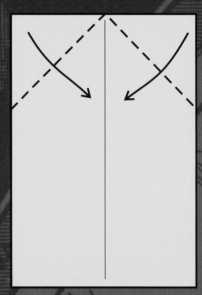

Fold the top two corners down to meet at the middle crease.

3

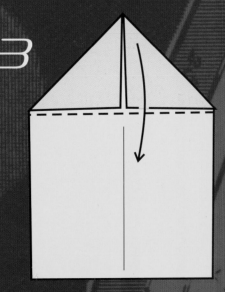

Fold the top point down, creasing just below the flap edges.

4

Fold in the top two corners to meet at the middle crease.

Stephen Weiss ©

5

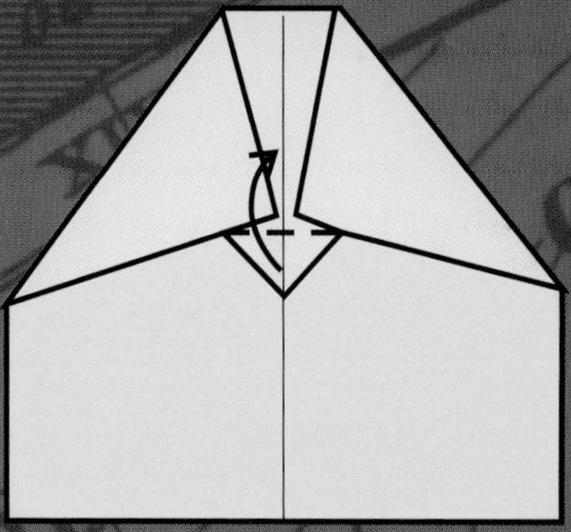

Fold the middle point up.

6

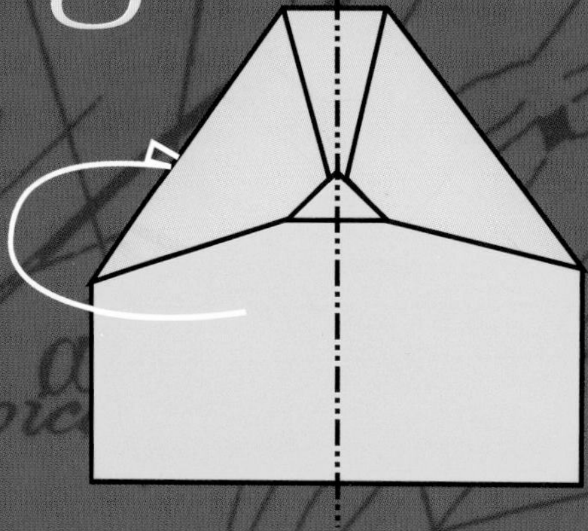

Mountain fold the plane in half.

7

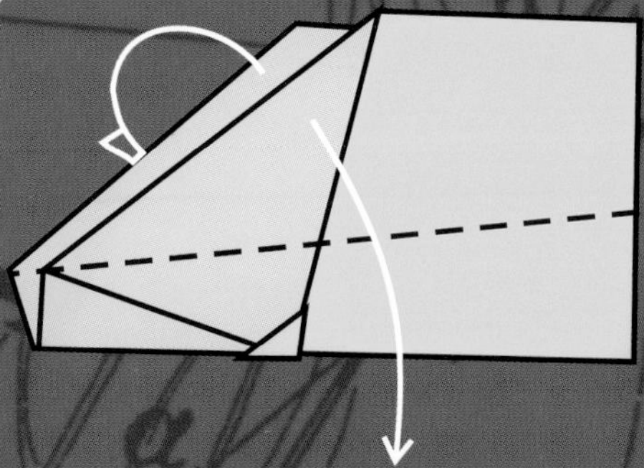

Fold both wings down.

TIP: Horizontal launching results in steady flights and is best for delicate gliders.

8

Ready for flight!

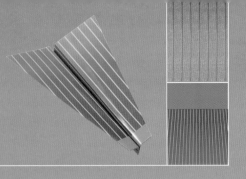

Straight and Narrow

A versatile indoor and outdoor flier, simple and reliable.

1

Side One

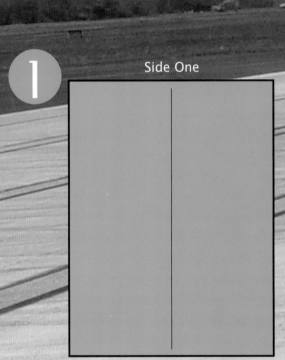

Fold and unfold to create a vertical middle crease.

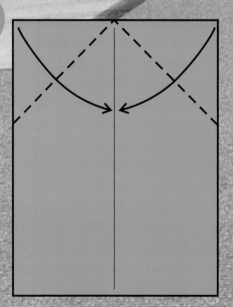

2

Fold the top two corners down to meet at the middle crease.

TIP: Always fold on a hard surface, neatly and accurately. Use the side of a ruler to make your creases sharp.

Stephen Weiss

14

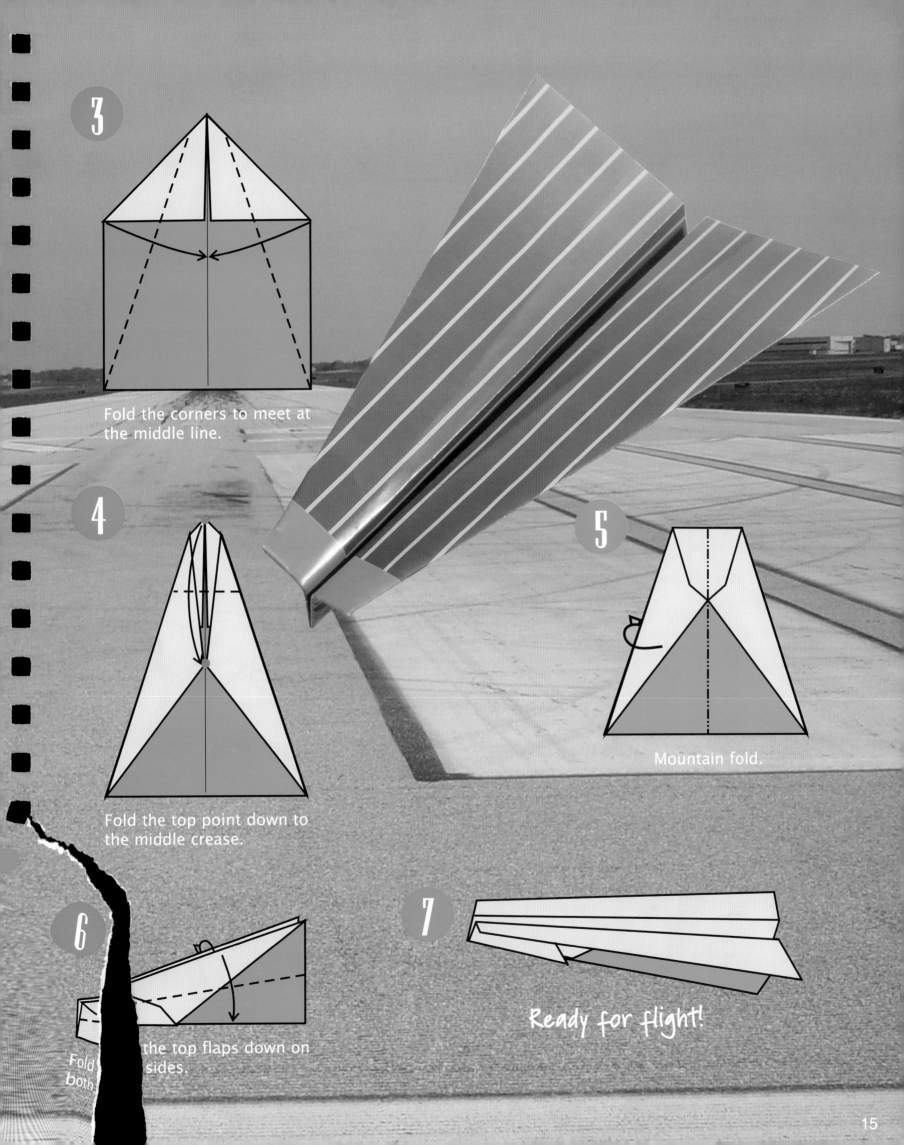

3

Fold the corners to meet at the middle line.

4

Fold the top point down to the middle crease.

5

Mountain fold.

6

Fold the top flaps down on both sides.

7

Ready for flight!

Plane Name: Dart Nose

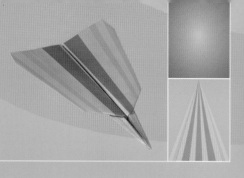

Dart Nose

A modern and fresh variation on the classic dart.
An indoor and outdoor flier.

1

Side One

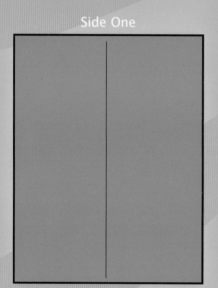

Fold and unfold to create
a vertical middle crease.

2

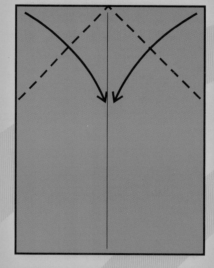

Fold the top corners down
to meet at the middle crease.

3

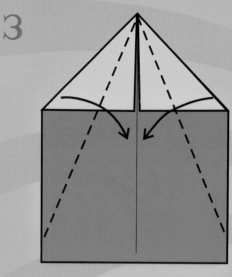

Fold the corners to meet
at the middle line.

4

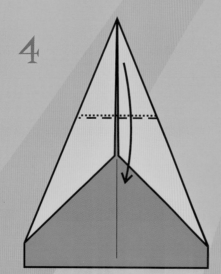

Fold the top point down
along the hidden edges
(X-ray line).

5

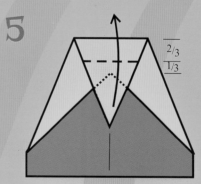

2/3
1/3

Fold the point up with a creas
one third of the way between   e
intersection of the hidden edg   the
(X-ray line) and the top edge.   es

16

Stephen Weiss

FACT:
Aerogami is a form of origami, the Japanese art of paper folding.

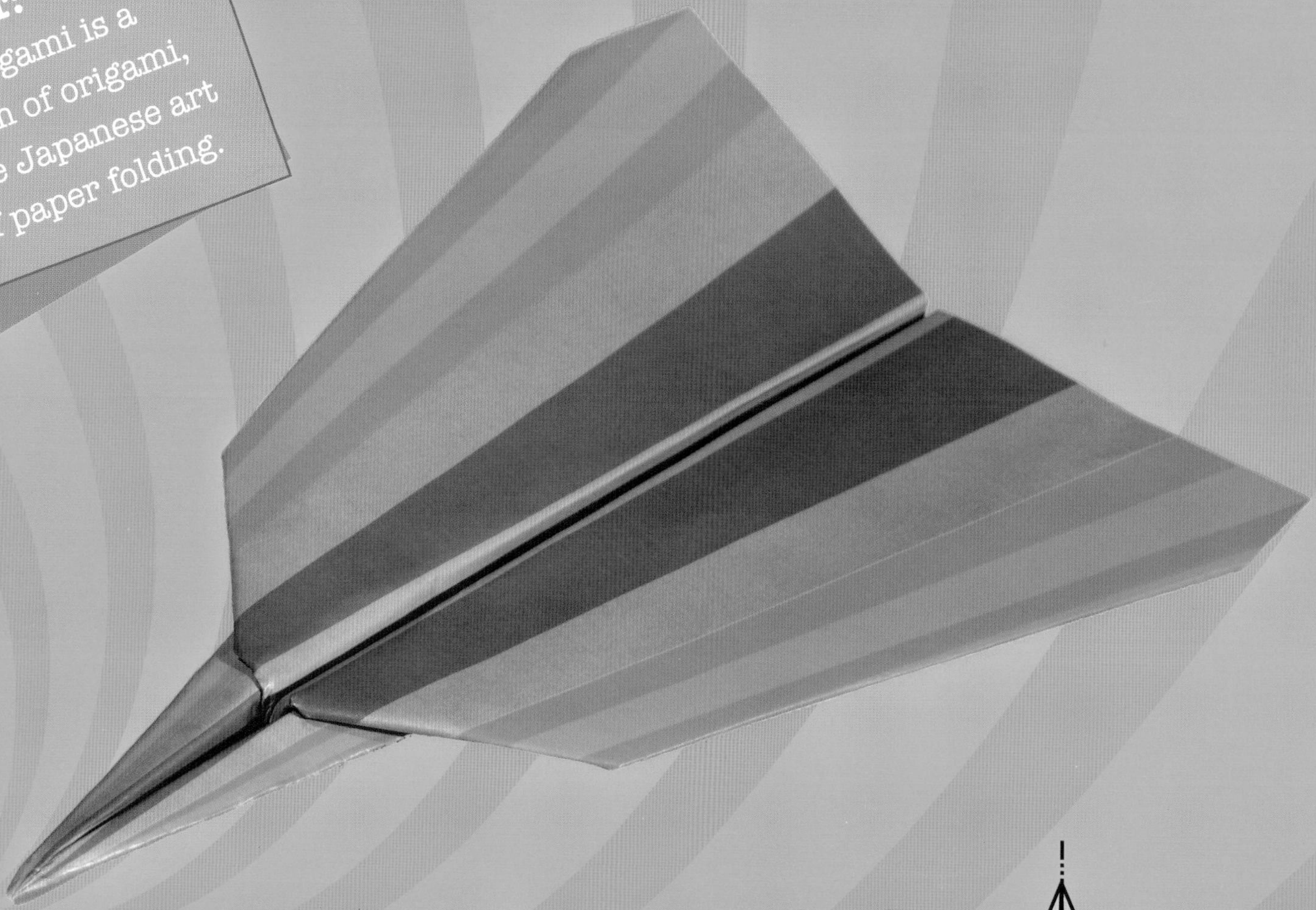

6

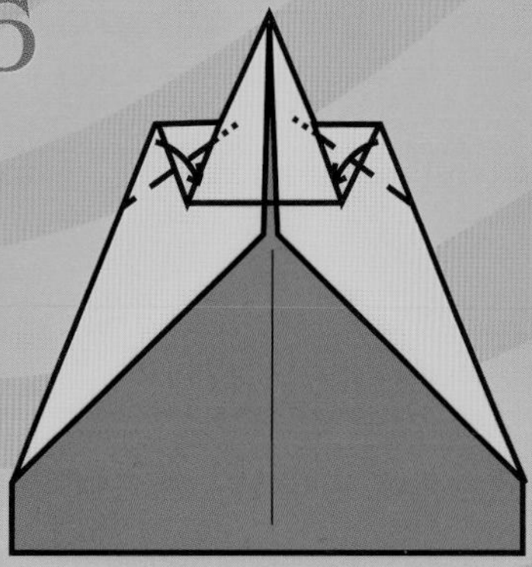

Tuck right and left corners down behind the point.

7

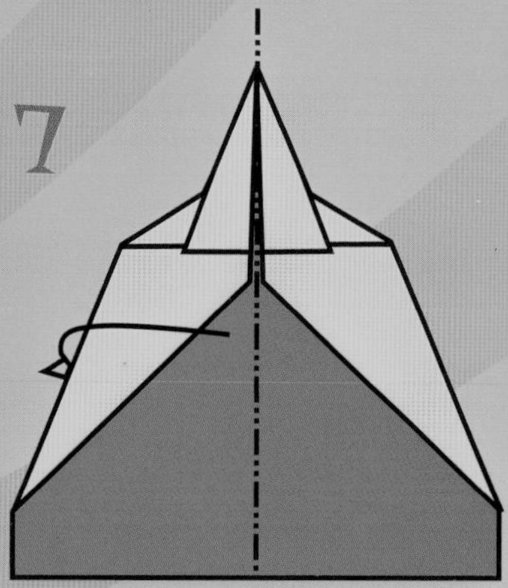

Mountain fold the plane down the middle crease.

8

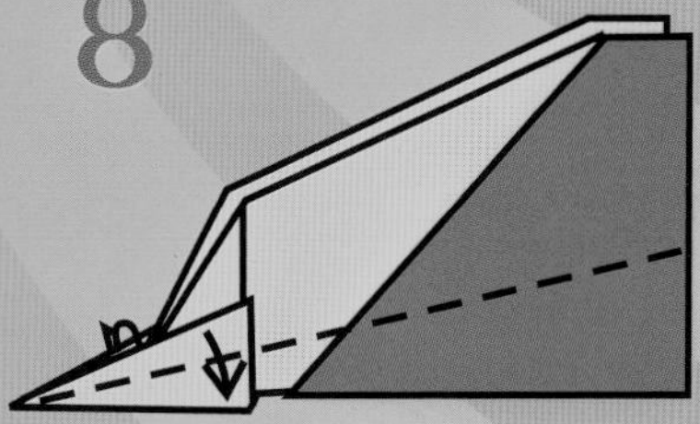

Fold the wings down on both sides.

9

Ready for flight!

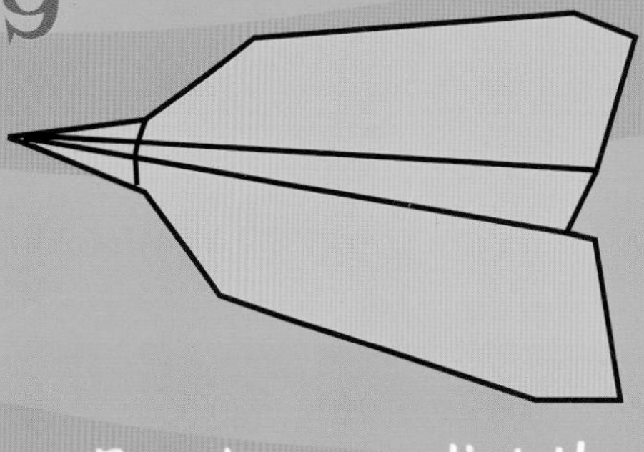

Fly Paper

An asymmetrical paper plane you hold and launch conventionally!

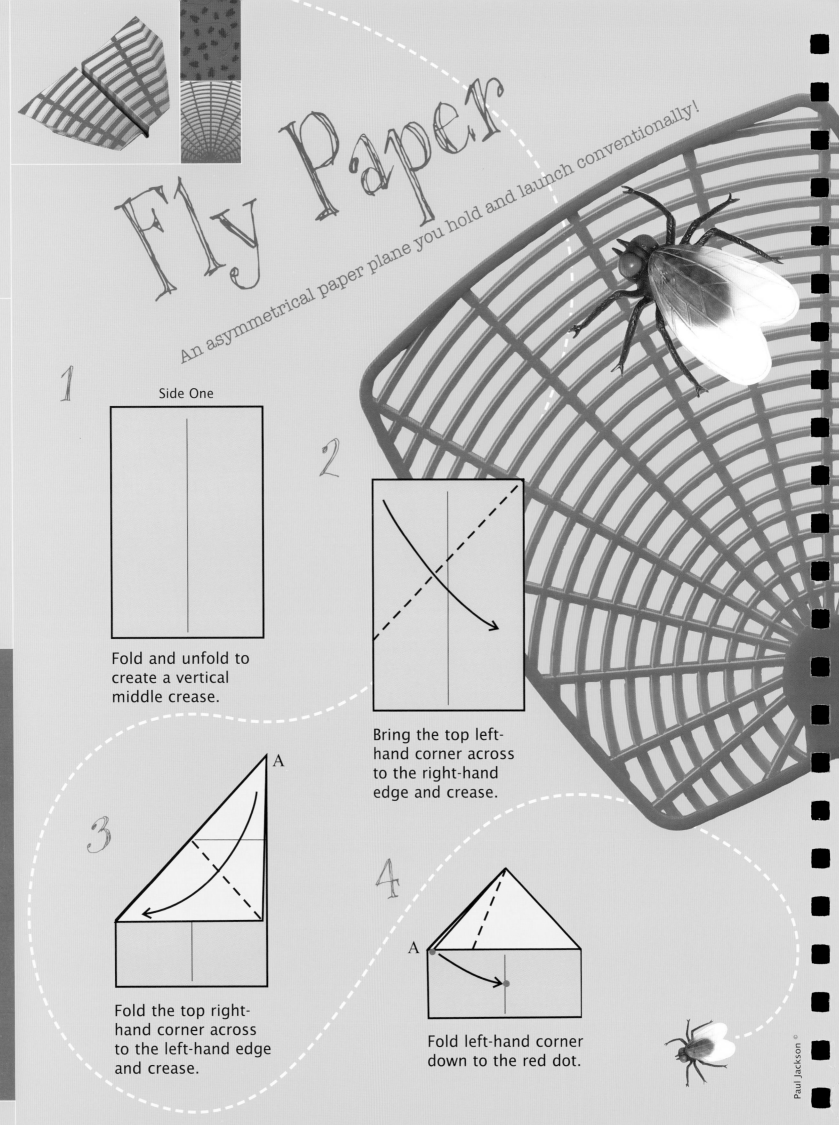

1

Side One

Fold and unfold to create a vertical middle crease.

2

Bring the top left-hand corner across to the right-hand edge and crease.

3

A

Fold the top right-hand corner across to the left-hand edge and crease.

4

A

Fold left-hand corner down to the red dot.

5

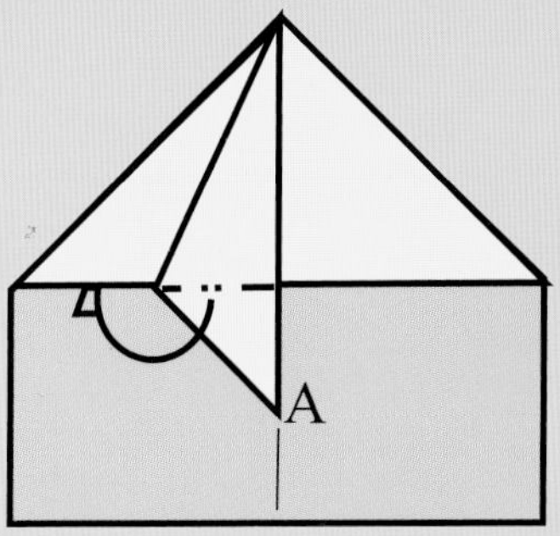

Tuck corner A out
of sight.

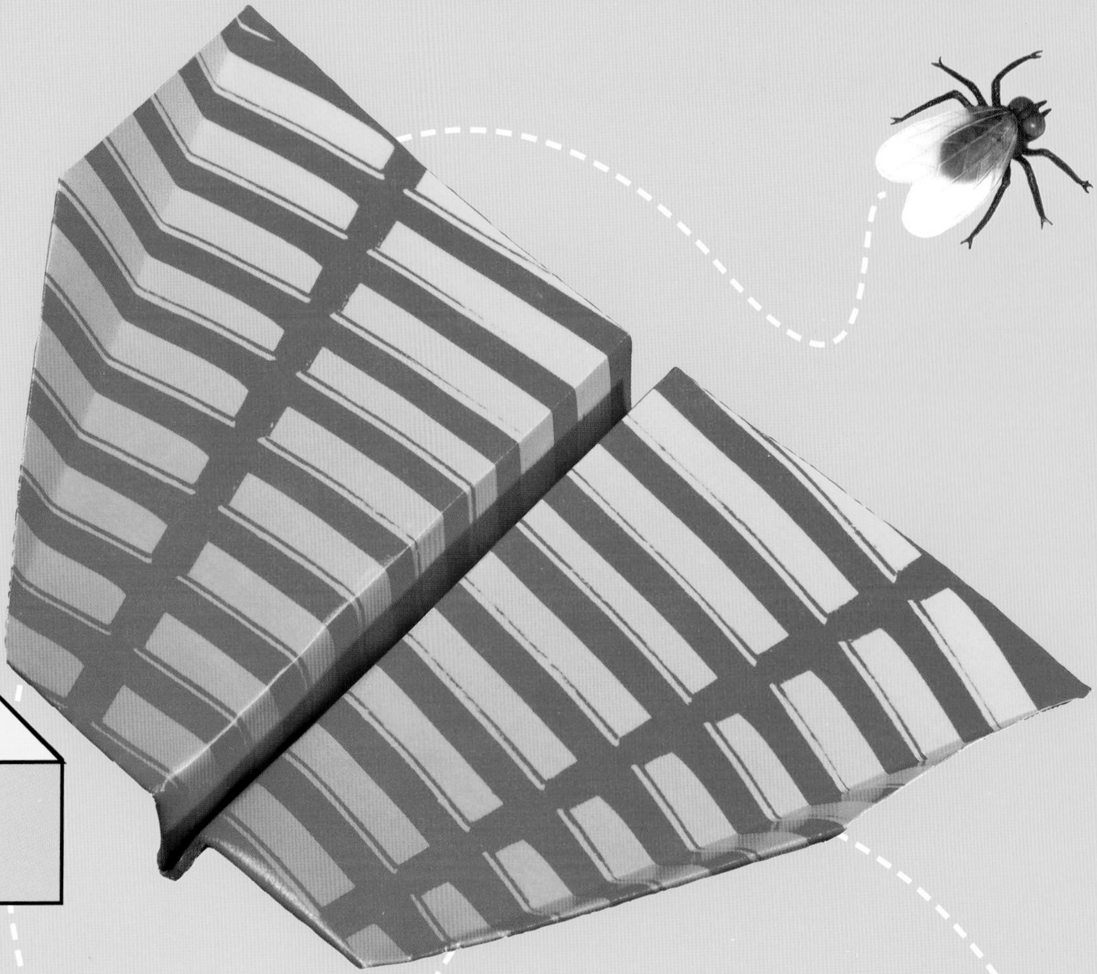

A

6

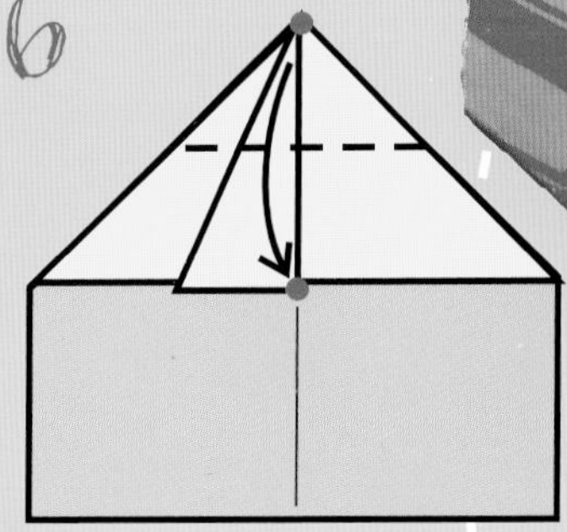

Fold dot to dot.

7

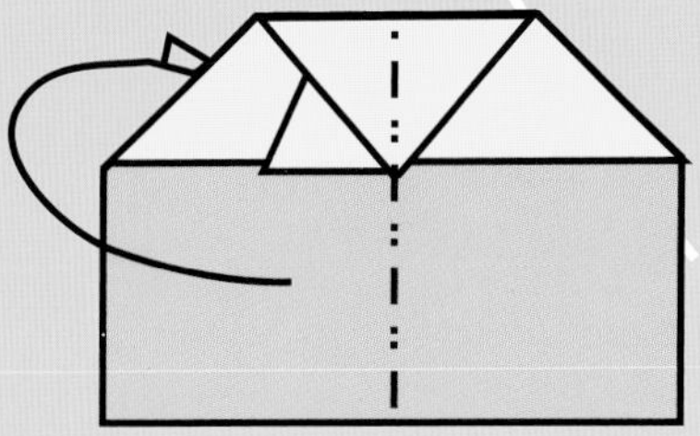

Mountain fold the
paper in half.

8

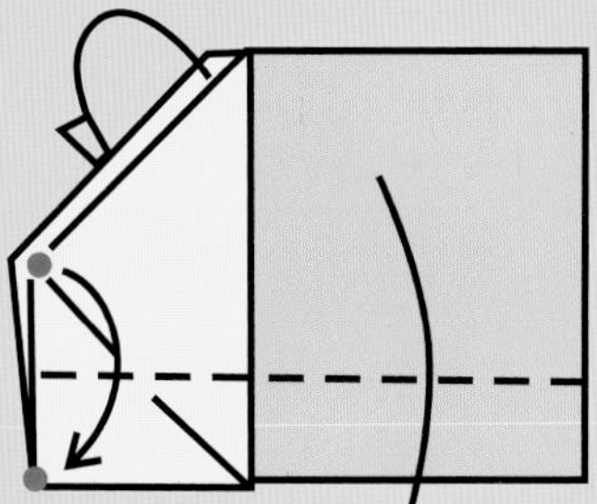

Fold dot to dot as
shown, so that the
crease is parallel to
the bottom edge.
Repeat behind.

9

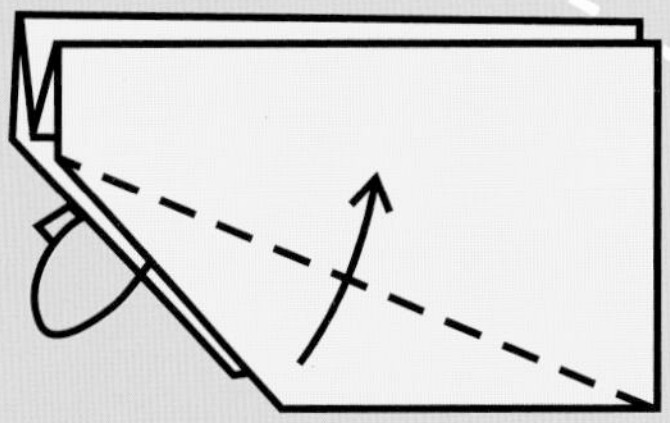

Fold up the leading
edge of the wing.
Repeat behind.

10

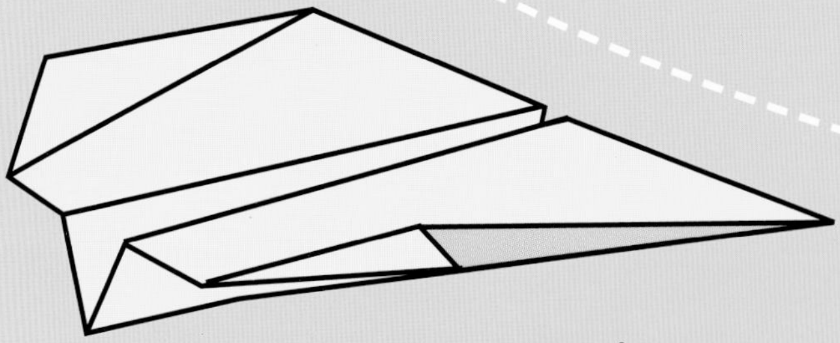

Ready for flight!

Level of diffic

Type of plane: glider

Plane Name: Triumph

THIS INDOOR AND OUTDOOR FLIER BOASTS A CLEAN AND
ELEGANT DESIGN.

1

Side One

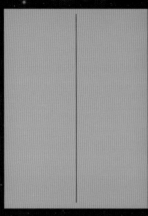

Fold and unfold to
create a vertical
middle crease.

2

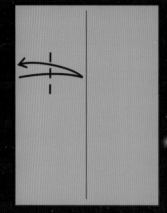

Crease and unfold.

3

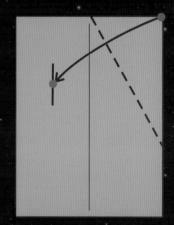

Fold right corner
down, dot to dot.

4

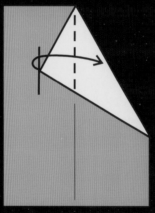

Valley fold flap to
right edge of paper.

5

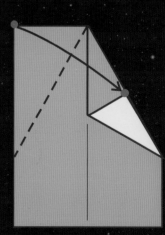

Valley fold top left
corner down, dot
to dot.

Stephen Weiss ©

6

Fold top layer over
to left edge of paper.

7

Fold tip of paper
down, dot to dot.

8

Fold down sides to
meet at the red dot.

9

Fold small point in
the middle up over
side flaps.

10

Pleat as shown and
turn the plane over.

11

Ready for flight.

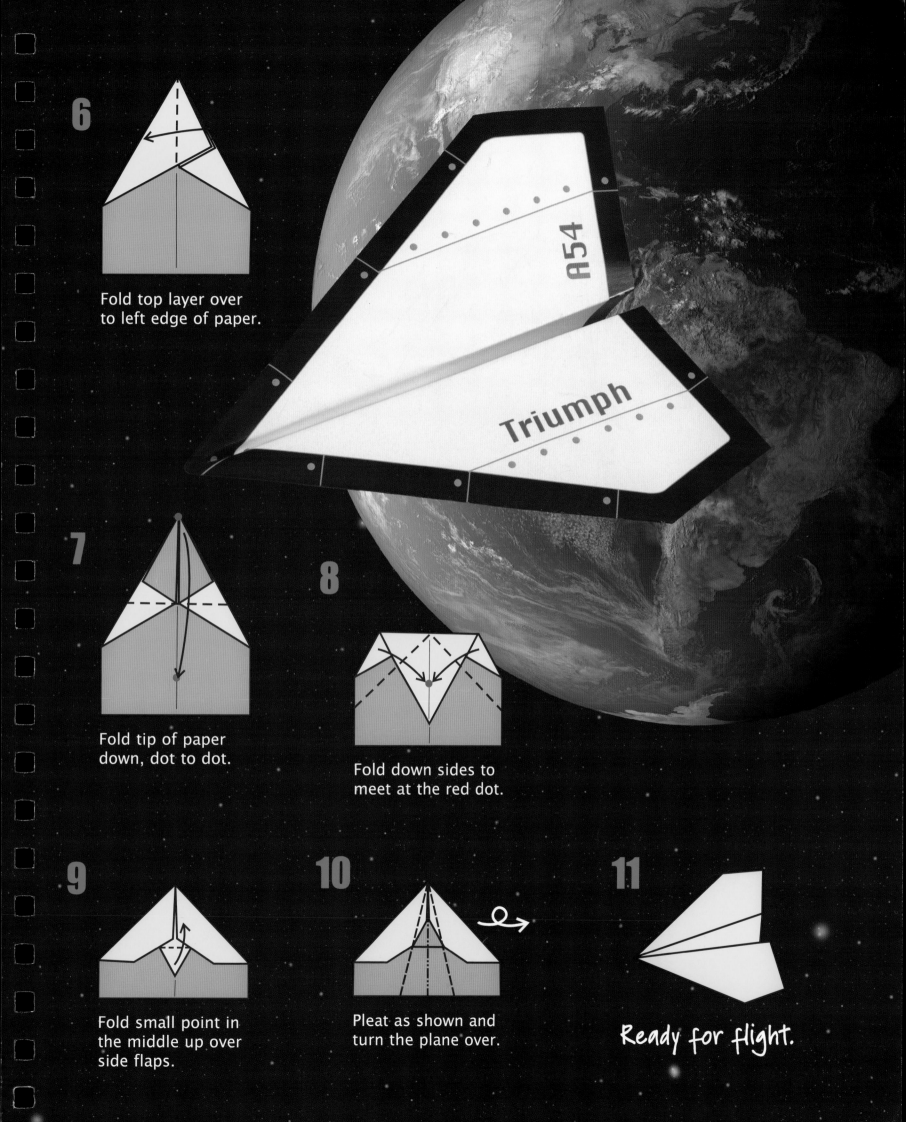

Troubleshooting Techniques

You may encounter problems when flying your paper plane. Park your plane in our hangar and test out the following techniques to help your plane fly properly.

Read the folding instructions carefully. A missed step or incorrect fold may spell disaster when flying your plane.

Small adjustments often help paper planes fly properly. First, make sure all edges and surfaces are as symmetrical as possible.

If the plane rises, stalls, and drops, try curving the rear edges or corners slightly downward.

If a plane nose dives towards the floor, try curving the rear edges or corners slightly upward.

Some planes fly better with a soft throw, while others need a harder throw, and some models can be thrown either way. An outdoor breeze may be all some planes need to become airborne.

Raising or lowering the wings evenly on both sides can also affect flight.

COMPASS

If all of your tweaking still results in a wobbly flight, try refolding it with a new sheet of paper.

33 0 3 6 9 12 30 27

Feather

Toss it around, it can take it!
This handsome plane is a fast flier.

1

Side One

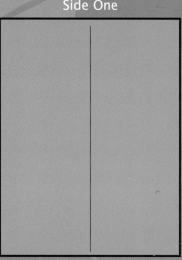

Fold and unfold to create
a vertical middle crease.

2

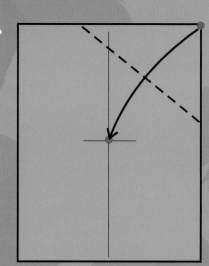

Make a horizontal crease
mark in the middle of the
paper; then fold the top
right corner, dot to dot.

3

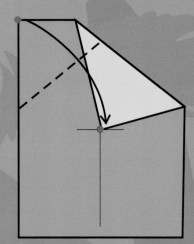

Repeat the Valley
fold on the left side
of the paper.

4

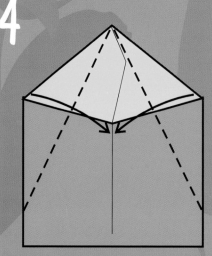

Fold the upper edges in
to the middle crease.

Stephen Weiss ©

5

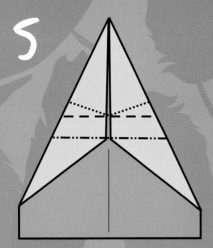

Note the X-ray view lines for hidden layers. Make a Valley fold across the upper reference point. Then make a Mountain fold across the lower reference point.

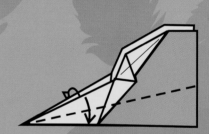

6

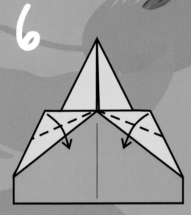

Fold the corners down as far as possible.

7

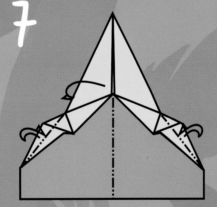

Mountain fold and unfold the side flaps. Then Mountain fold the model in half.

8

Fold down the wing. Repeat behind.

TIP: Throw dart planes straight or at an upward, 45-degree angle.

9

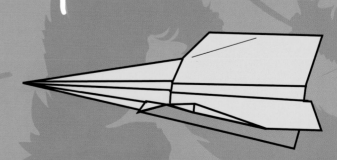

Ready for flight!

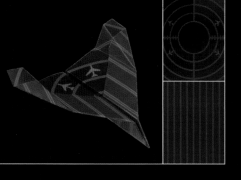

Delta Wing

Its simple triangular shape flies high!

1

Side One

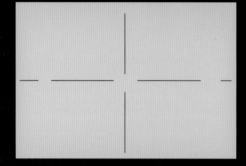

Fold and unfold to create both vertical and horizontal middle creases.

2

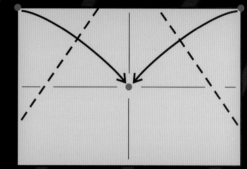

Fold the top corners down to meet at the middle red dot.

3

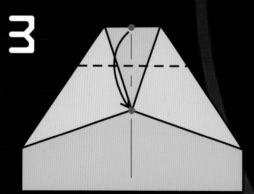

Valley fold down, dot to dot.

4

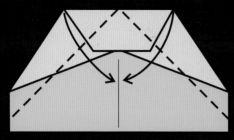

Fold down top corners to meet at the middle crease.

5

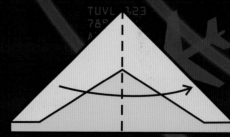

Valley fold the plane vertically in half.

Paul Jackson ©

6

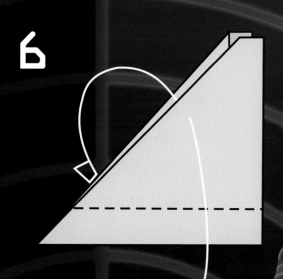

Horizontally fold the wing
down at the reference line.
Repeat for opposite side.

TIP:
Make sure you
fold Steps 5 to
7 carefully and
throw the plane
with moderate
force.

7

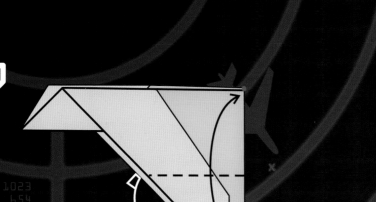

IHF 1023
456 654
XYZ LAX

Fold tip of wing up, dot to dot.
Repeat for opposite side.

8

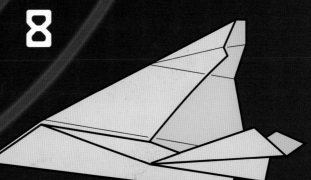

Ready for flight!

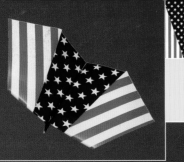

Albert Ross

Expansive wings help this plane soar both indoors and out. Launch with medium force for best results.

1

Side One

Fold and unfold to create a vertical middle crease.

2

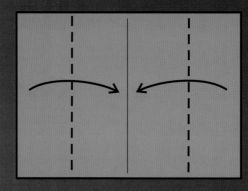

Fold left and right sides in to middle crease.

TIP:
Launch a glider with a smooth, even motion.

3

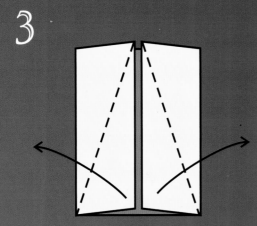

Valley fold inside flaps out to resemble image in Step 4.

4

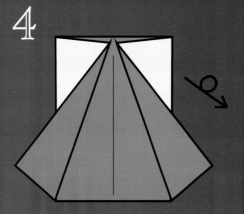

Flip over.

Paul Jackson ©

5

Fold top down horizontally dot to dot.

6

Fold top down horizontally, dot to dot.

7

Valley fold top down at reference line.

8

Mountain fold down the middle of the plane. Then, use Valley folds to create the wings.

9

Ready for flight!

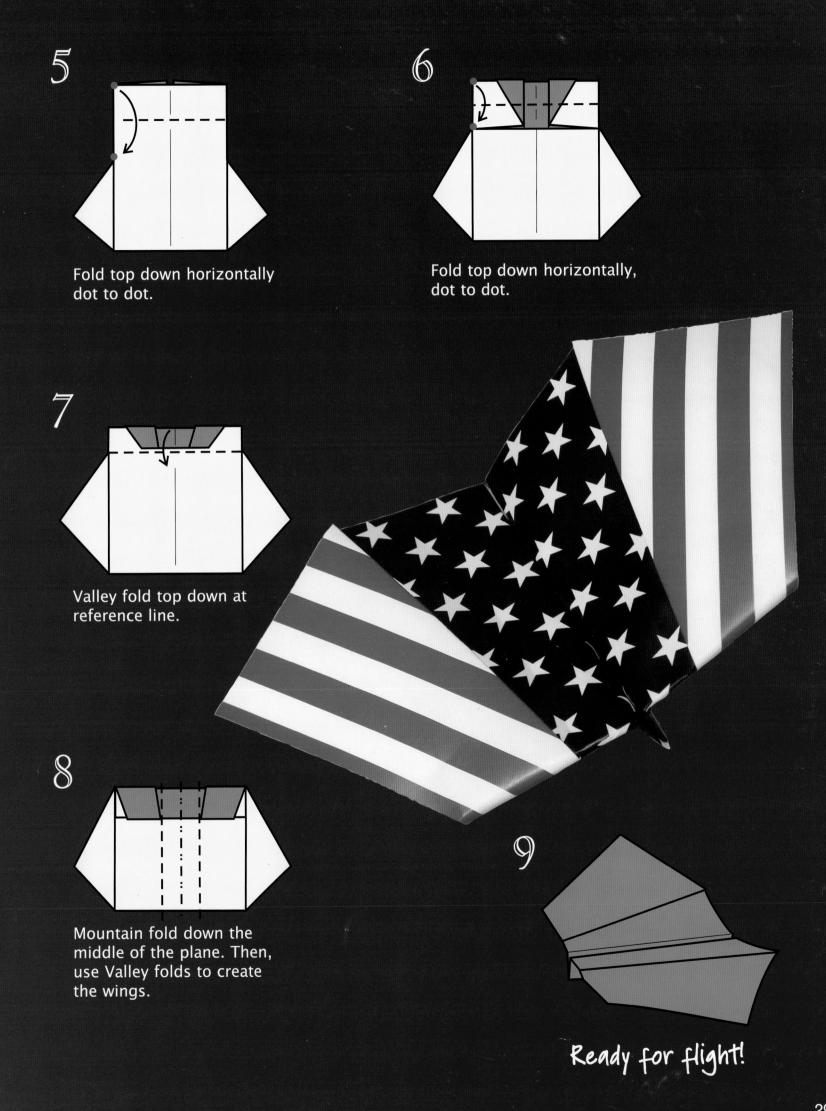

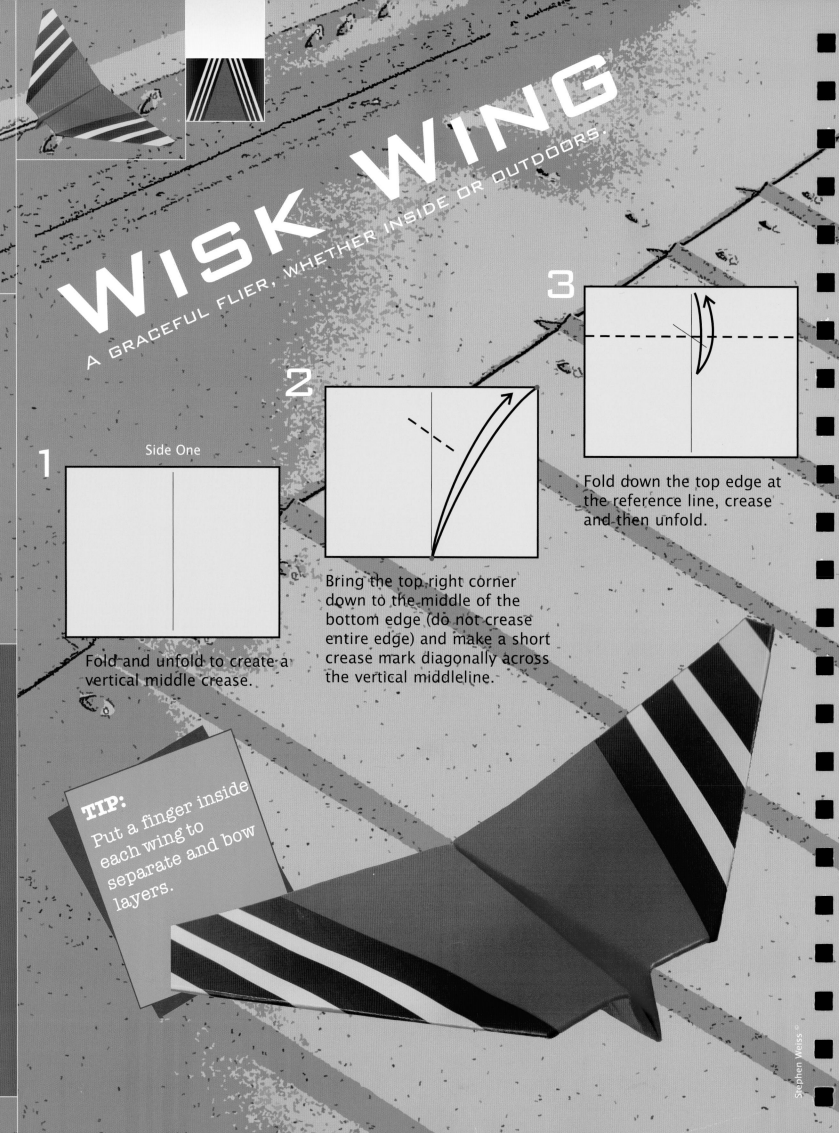

WISK WING

A GRACEFUL FLIER, WHETHER INSIDE OR OUTDOORS.

1

Side One

Fold and unfold to create a vertical middle crease.

2

Bring the top right corner down to the middle of the bottom edge (do not crease entire edge) and make a short crease mark diagonally across the vertical middleline.

3

Fold down the top edge at the reference line, crease and then unfold.

TIP:
Put a finger inside each wing to separate and bow layers.

Stephen Weiss ©

4

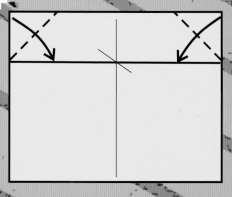

Fold in the top corners to the crease.

5

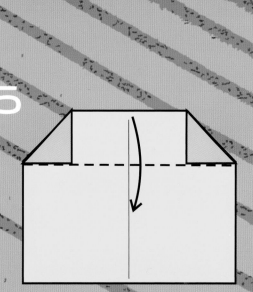

Fold the top of the paper down to the middle crease.

6

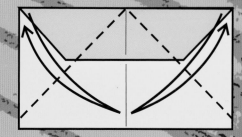

Bring the top corners down to meet at the bottom of the page; unfold.

7

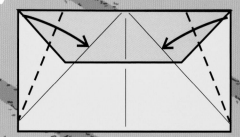

Valley fold the right and left corners down to the crease made in Step 6.

8

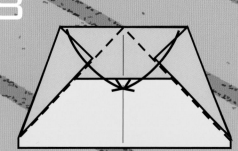

Fold corners down to meet at the middle crease.

9

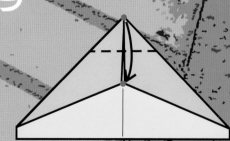

Bring point down to the red dot.

10

Mountain fold plane at the middle vertical.

11

Fold the wing down, matching the red dots. Repeat behind.

12

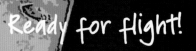

Ready for flight!

SKY BARGE

THE CLEAN AND EFFICIENT DESIGN YIELDS SMOOTH, PLEASING FLIGHTS.

1
Side One

Fold and unfold to create both vertical and horizontal middle creases.

2

Fold top edge down to the middle crease and unfold.

3

Fold both top corners down to the first crease.

4

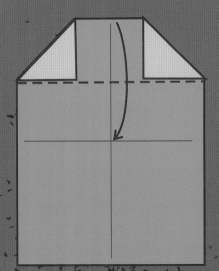

Fold the top down to the middle crease.

Stephen Weiss ®

5

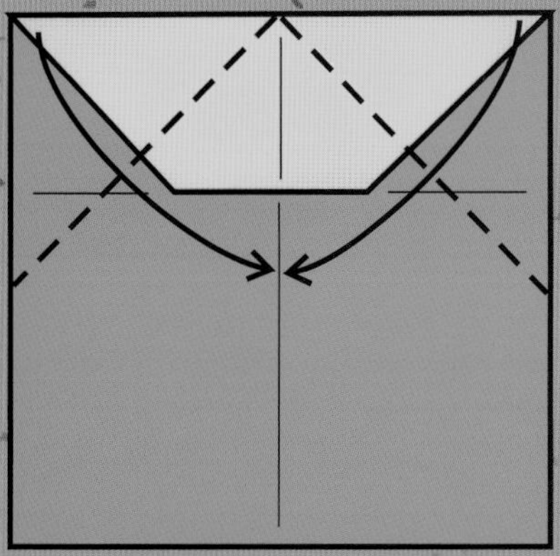

Fold both top corners down
to meet at the middle crease.

6

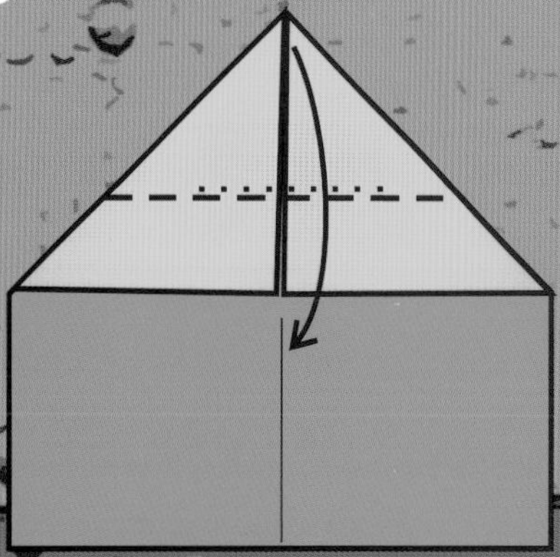

Fold the top point down
along the hidden edge
(X-ray line).

7

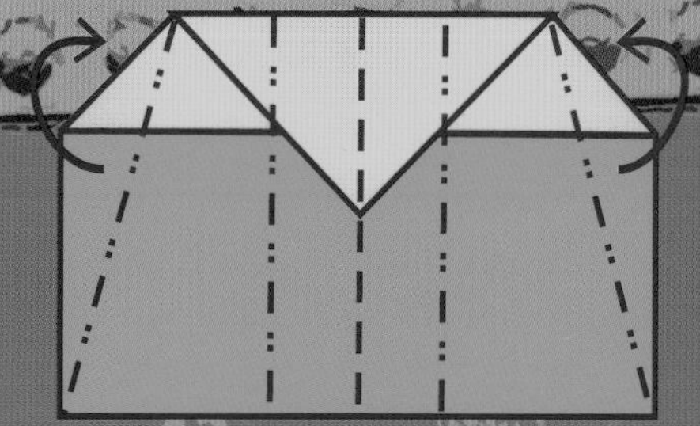

Form the final shape.
The side flaps should be
bent down at 90 degrees
to the wings.

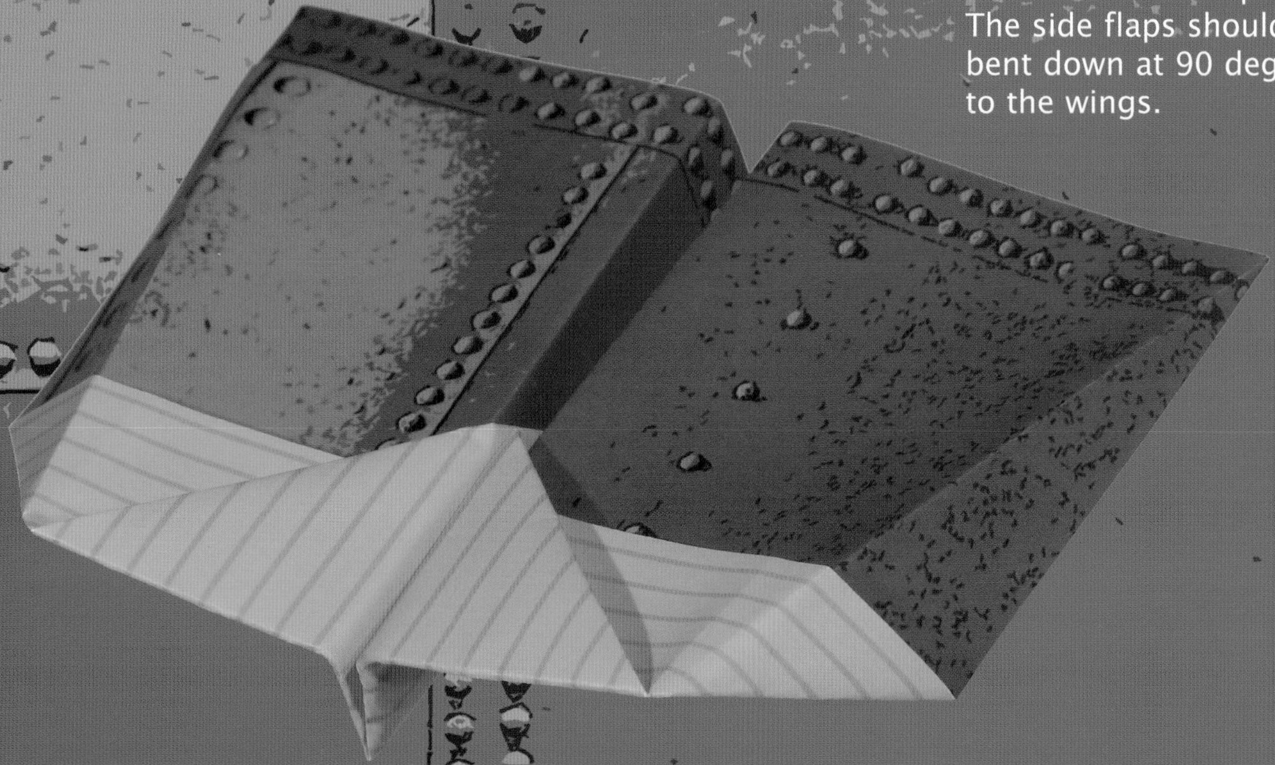

Front View

8

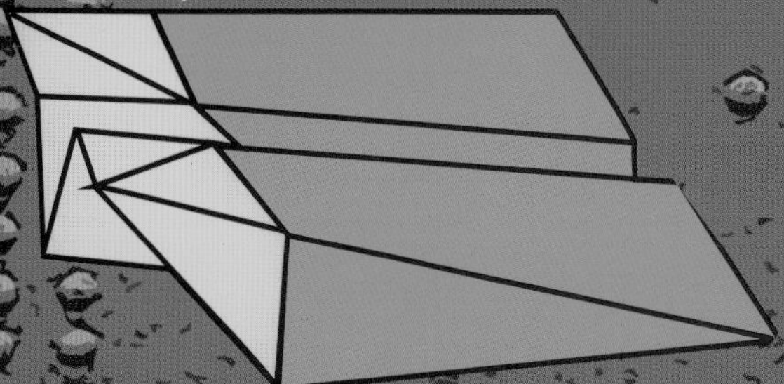

Ready for flight!

Type of plane: glider

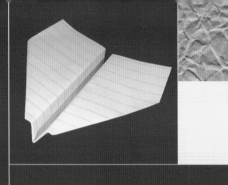

CLASSROOM CRUISER

Why mess with a classic? This perfectly balanced plane is built for distance. Use notebook paper or your bag from lunch.

1

Side One

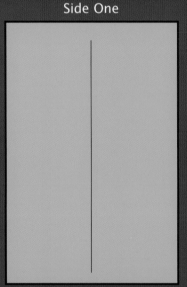

Fold and unfold to create a vertical middle crease.

2

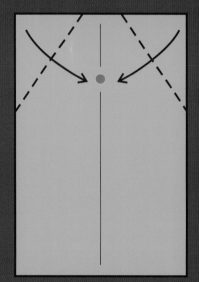

Fold top corners down to red dot.

3

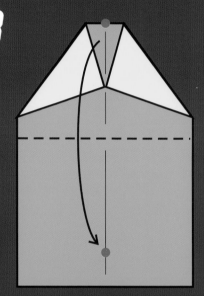

Fold dot to dot, approximately 1 inch (2.5 cm) from bottom.

4

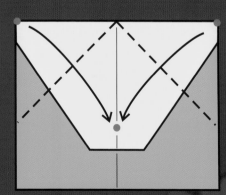

Bring top corners down to the middle red dot.

TIP:
The four main angles of launch are vertically upward, diagonally upward, horizontal, and downward.

Paul Jackson ®

5

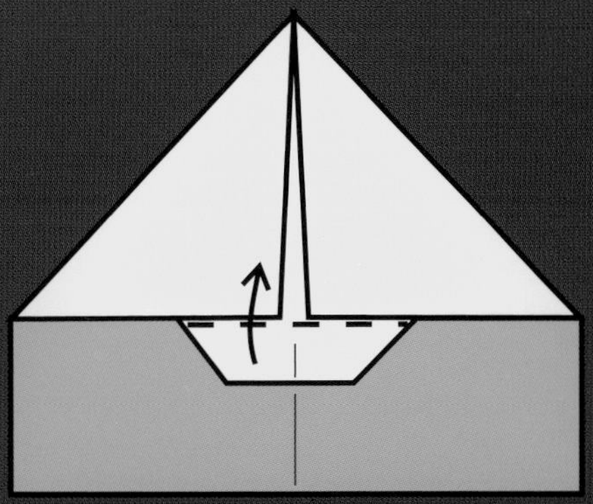

Fold the middle flap up.

6

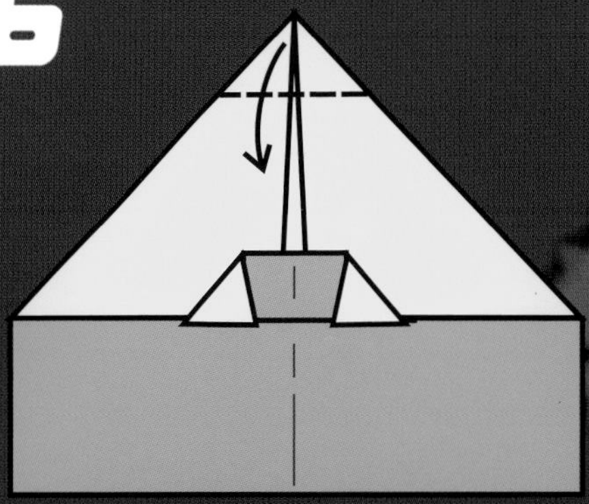

Fold the tip down.

7

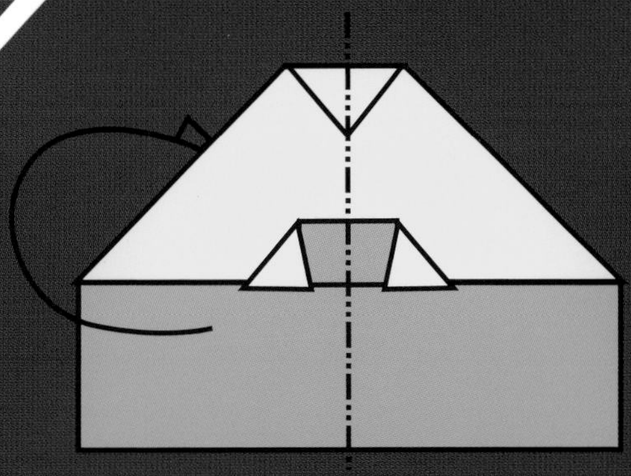

Mountain fold the plane
in half.

8

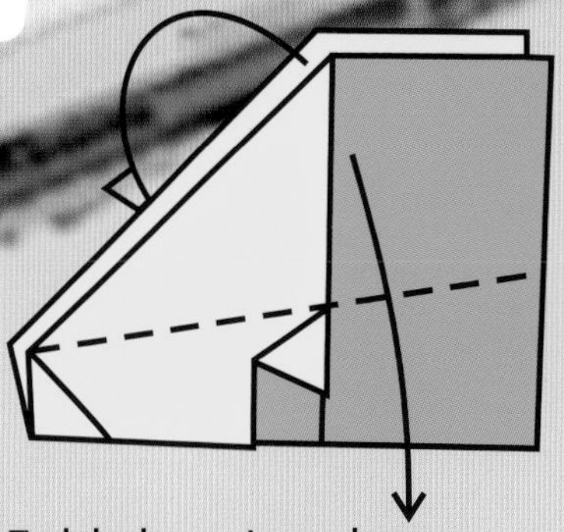

Fold the wing down.
Repeat behind.

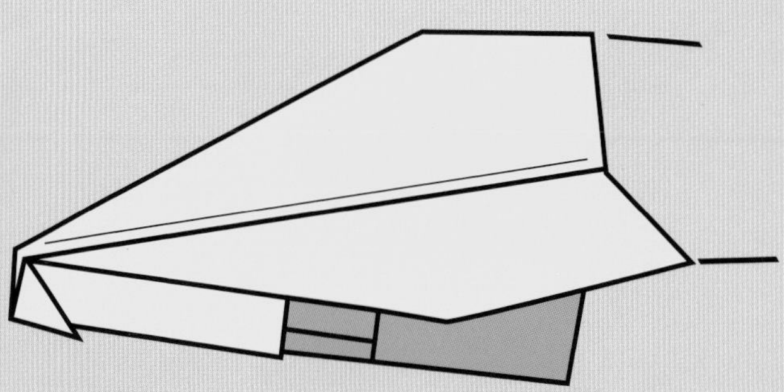

Ready for flight!

hoop-nosed scooter

unusual in looks, but steady in performance.

1 Side One

Fold and unfold to create a vertical middle crease.

2 A B C D

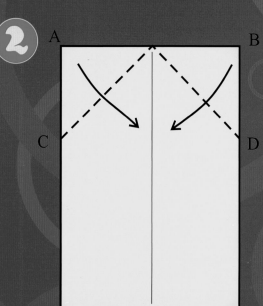

Fold corners A and B in to middle crease. Then, flip paper over.

3

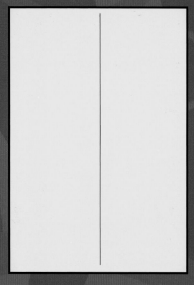

B A D C

Unfold corners A and B. Fold C and D in to middle crease.

4

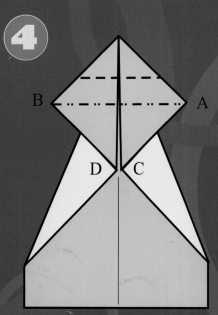

B A D C

Valley fold top point down.

Paul Jackson ©

5

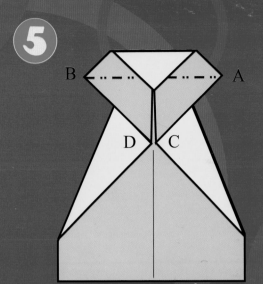

Mountain fold at corners A and B.

6

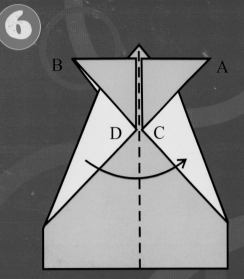

Valley fold the plane in half.

7

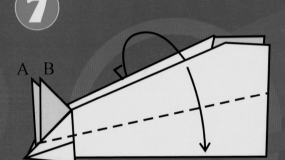

Fold the wing down. Repeat behind.

TIP:
Good flight depends on careful adjustment of the trailing edges, which usually need a slight upward bend.

8

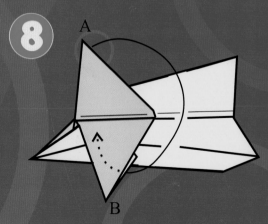

Tuck corner A inside corner B.

9

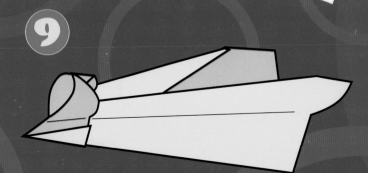

Ready for flight!

CANARD

THIS TYPE OF PLANE HAS A STABILIZER
IN FRONT OF THE WINGS.

1

Side One

Fold and unfold to create
a vertical middle crease.

2

Fold top right corner
down, dot to dot.

3

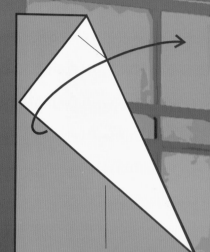

Unfold and repeat Step
2 on the other side.

4

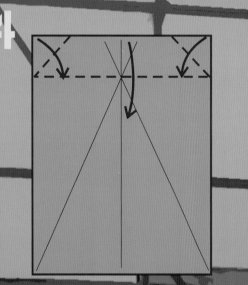

First, make the
horizontal crease, then
fold in the corners.

5

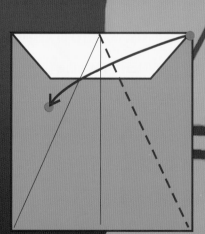

Bring top right corner
down, dot to dot.

Stephen Weiss ©

6

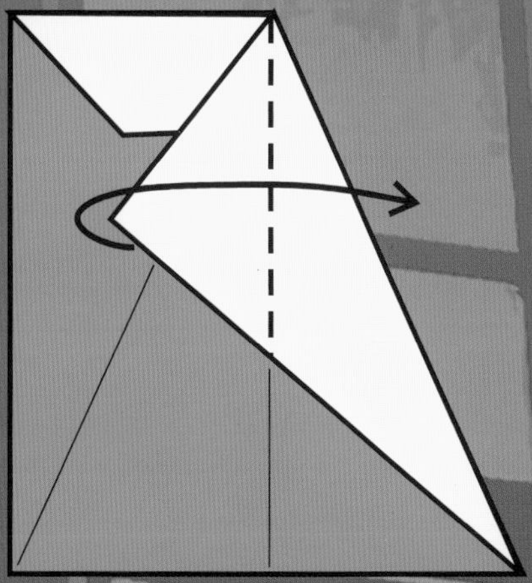

Valley fold top layer to the right.

7

Repeat steps 5 and 6 on the other side.

8

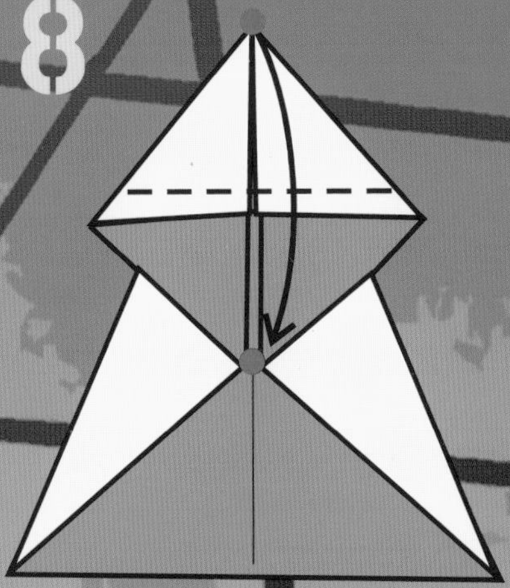

Valley fold, dot to dot.

9

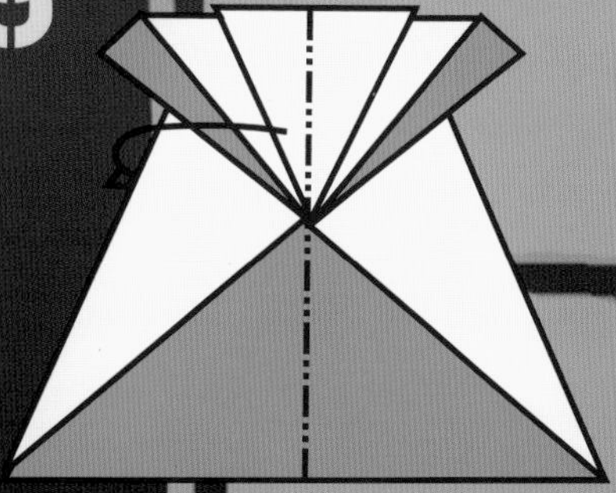

Mountain fold the plane in half.

10

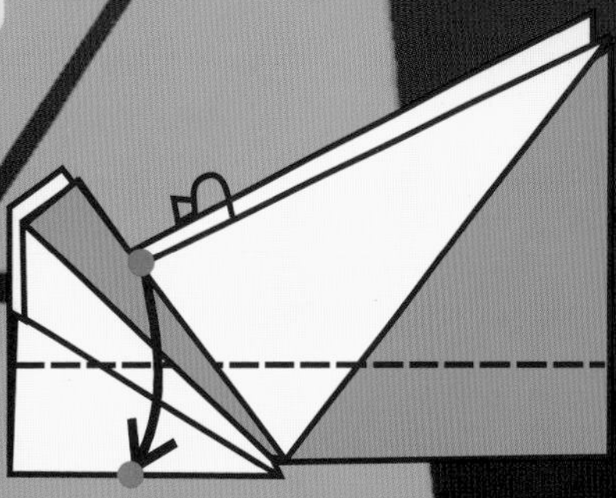

Valley fold the wings down, dot to dot.

11

Ready for flight!

Wind Hawk

A light breeze, indoors or out, is ideal for this plane. Try launching this plane into the wind—it should hover in the air.

1

Side One

Fold and unfold to create a vertical middle crease.

2

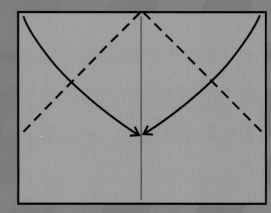

Fold corners in to middle crease.

3

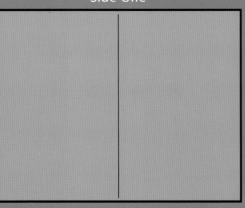

Again, fold outermost corners in to the middle crease.

4

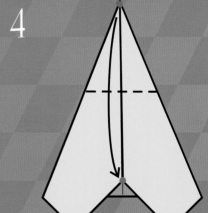

Valley fold point down to the red dot.

40

Stephen Weiss ©

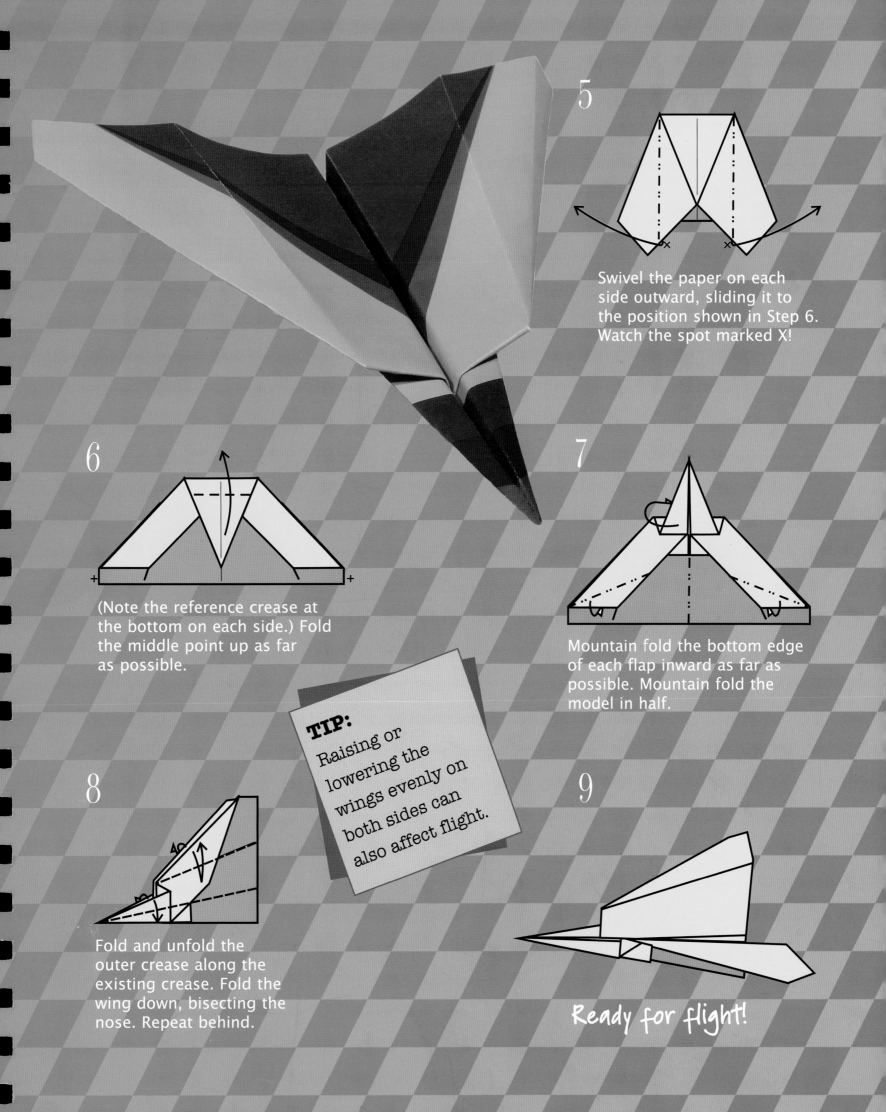

5

Swivel the paper on each side outward, sliding it to the position shown in Step 6. Watch the spot marked X!

6

(Note the reference crease at the bottom on each side.) Fold the middle point up as far as possible.

7

Mountain fold the bottom edge of each flap inward as far as possible. Mountain fold the model in half.

TIP:
Raising or lowering the wings evenly on both sides can also affect flight.

8

Fold and unfold the outer crease along the existing crease. Fold the wing down, bisecting the nose. Repeat behind.

9

Ready for flight!

Thunder Bomber

A traditional design that's simple to fold and easy to fly, what could be better?

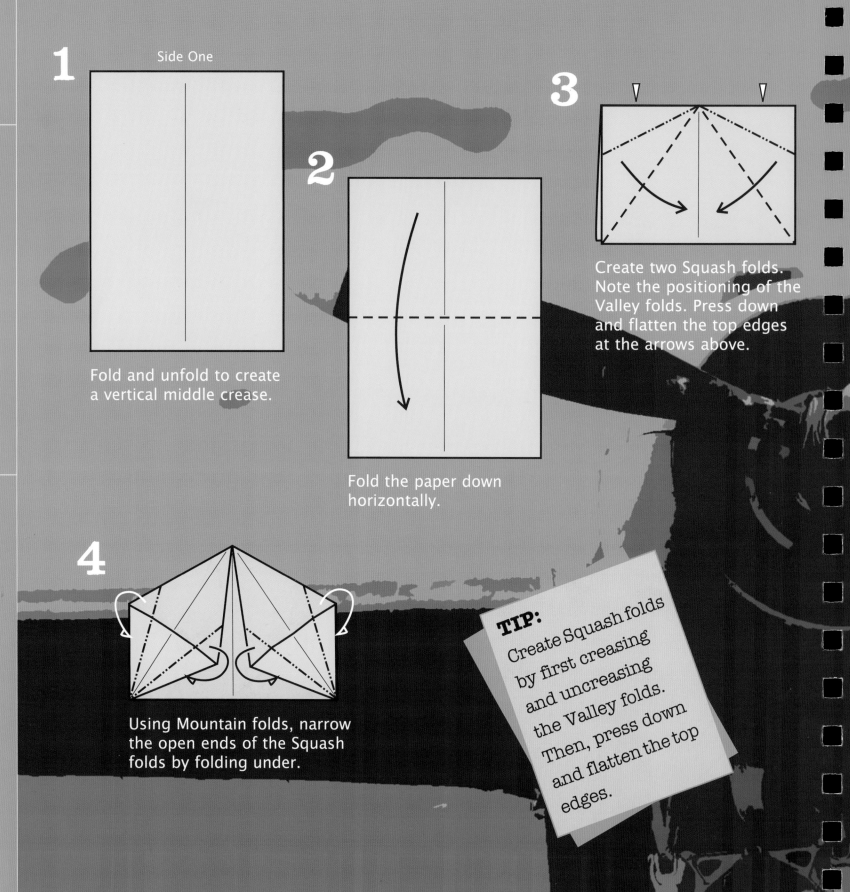

1

Side One

Fold and unfold to create a vertical middle crease.

2

Fold the paper down horizontally.

3

Create two Squash folds. Note the positioning of the Valley folds. Press down and flatten the top edges at the arrows above.

4

Using Mountain folds, narrow the open ends of the Squash folds by folding under.

TIP:
Create Squash folds by first creasing and uncreasing the Valley folds. Then, press down and flatten the top edges.

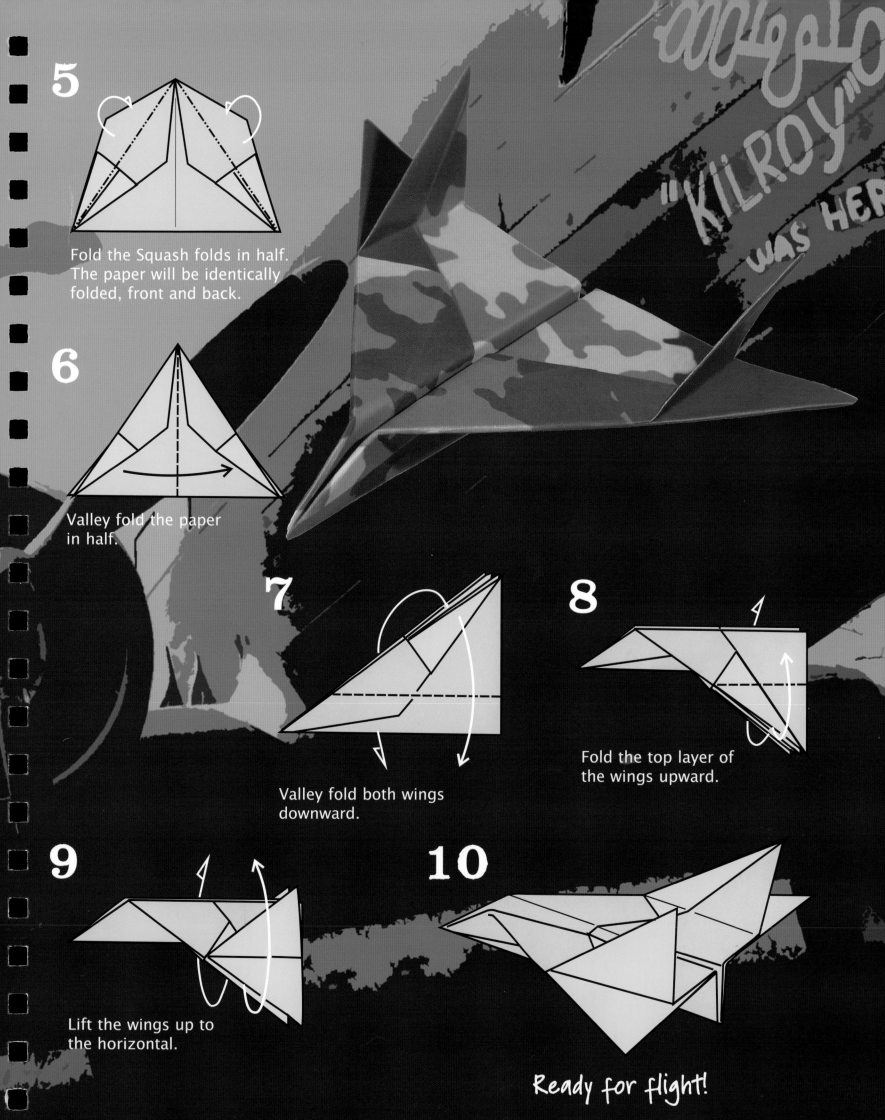

5

Fold the Squash folds in half. The paper will be identically folded, front and back.

6

Valley fold the paper in half.

7

Valley fold both wings downward.

8

Fold the top layer of the wings upward.

9

Lift the wings up to the horizontal.

10

Ready for flight!

43

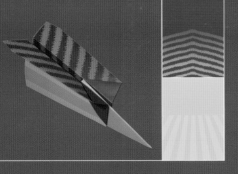

BULL'S-EYE DART
THIS IS A GREAT PLANE FOR TARGET GAMES.

1

Side One

Fold and unfold to create
a vertical middle crease.

2

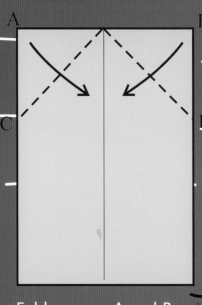

Fold corners A and B
in to middle crease.
Then, flip paper over.

3

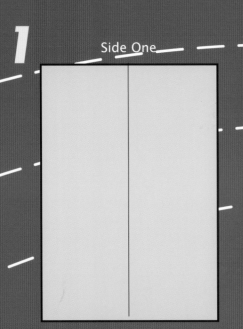

Unfold corners A and
B. Fold C and D in to
middle crease.

4

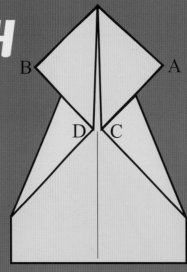

Flip over.

5

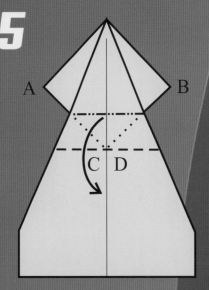

Make a Mountain fold
and a Valley fold across
the reference points.

44

Paul Jackson ©

6

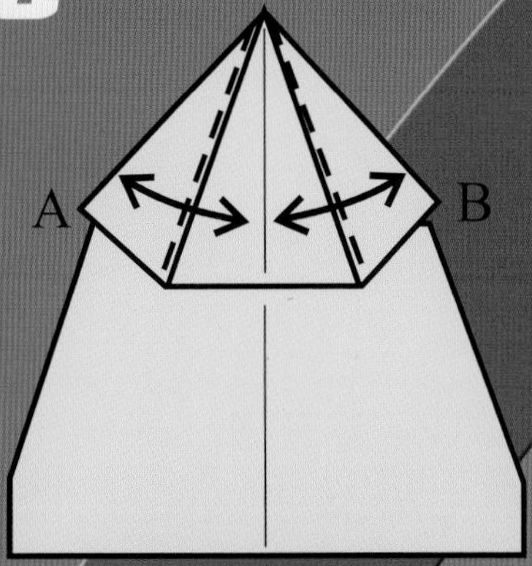

A ⟷ B

Fold A and B in to the middle crease, then unfold.

7

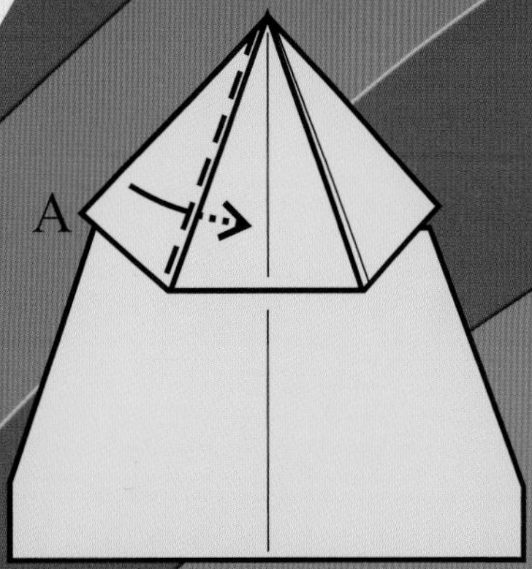

A

Tuck corner A inside the fold as shown.

8

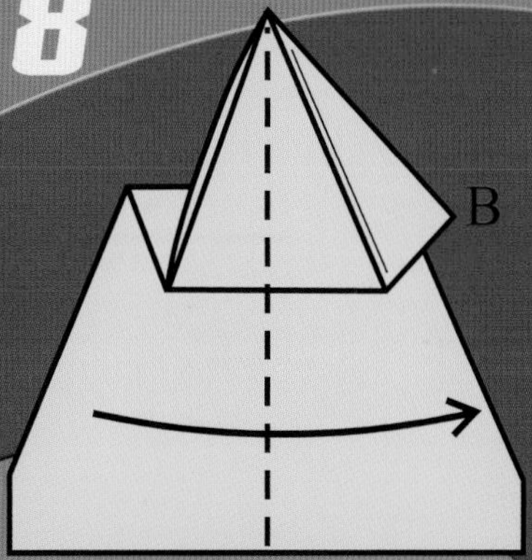

B

Valley fold model in half.

9

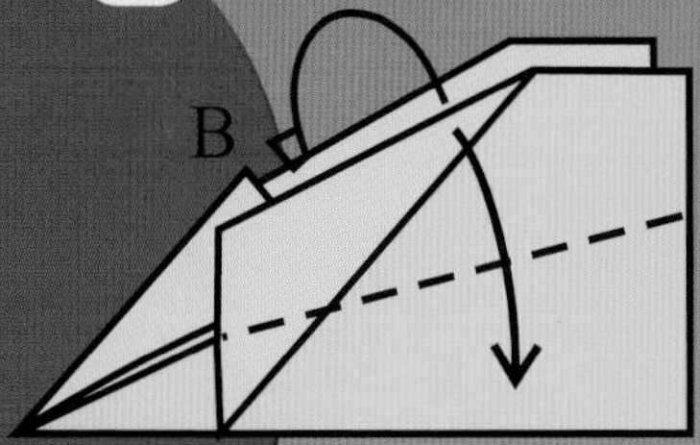

B

Fold wing down. Repeat behind.

10

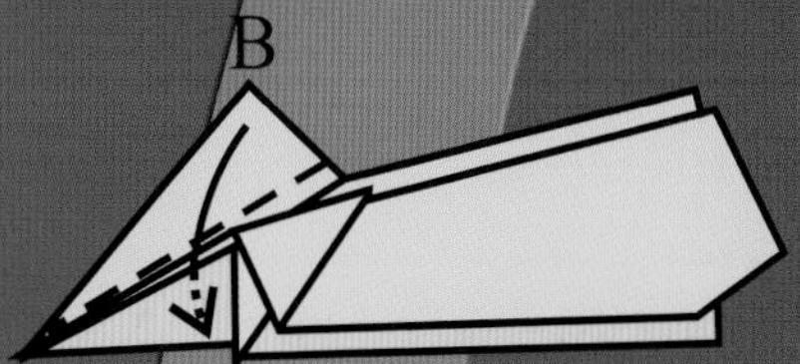

B

Tuck point B in to lock the nose.

11

Ready for flight!

FACT:
The earliest known date of using paper planes to test aerodynamics was said to have been in 1909.

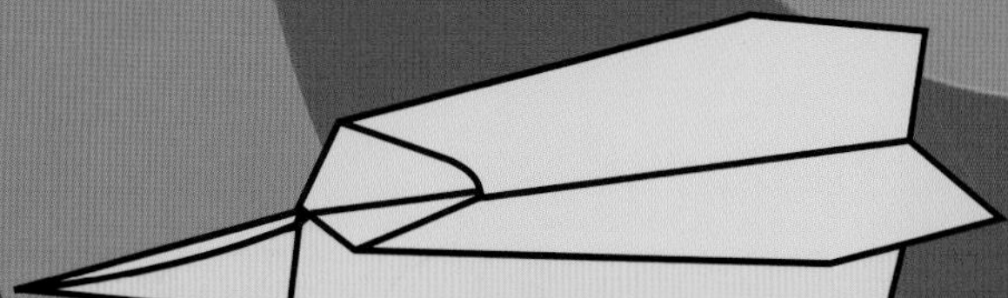

BREEZE

Compact and light, the Breeze works in all environments, but excels outdoors in a gentle current of air.

of plane: glider

1

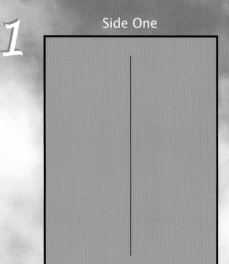

Side One

Fold and unfold to create
a vertical middle crease.

2

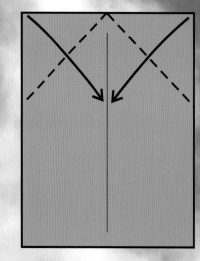

Fold left and right
corners in to the
middle crease.

3

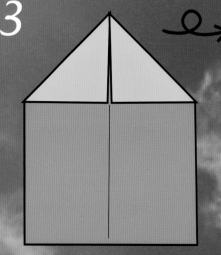

Turn the paper over.

TIP:
Curve the outside
rear corners
slightly upward.

4

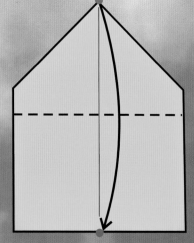

Fold model in half,
dot to dot.

5

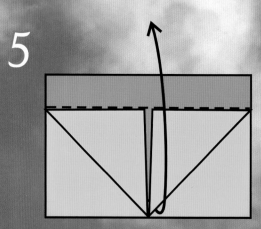

Valley fold the first layer.

Stephen Weiss ©

6

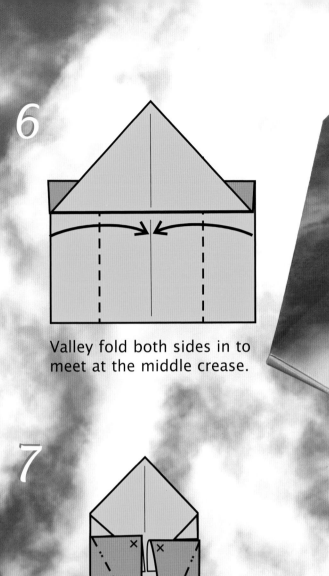

Valley fold both sides in to meet at the middle crease.

7

Open the flaps while flattening the top corners. (Note the position of the x marks in the next drawing.)

8

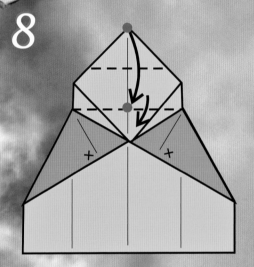

First, make the lower crease, then fold the top point to it.

9

Pleat as shown and turn the plane over.

10

Ready for flight!

FLAT FLYER

You'll get stable and fast flights if you throw it correctly.

1

Side One

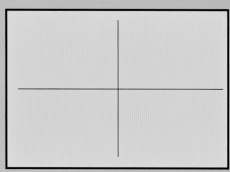

Fold and unfold to create both vertical and horizontal middle creases.

2

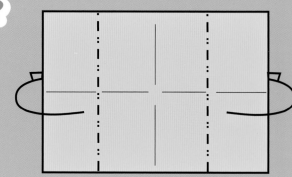

Mountain fold right and left sides to the middle crease.

3

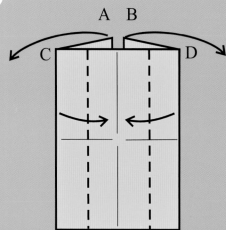

Turn in right and left sides at C and D to meet at middle crease. Corners A and B will become new corners.

4

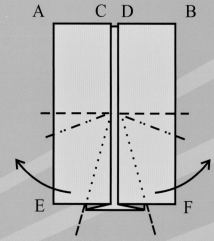

Pull corners E and F up and out, creating Mountain folds on both sides.

Paul Jackson®

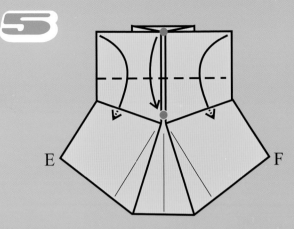

5

E   F

Fold down, dot to dot,
tucking corners under folds.

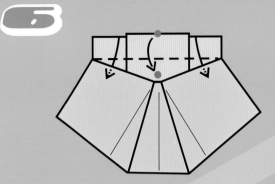

6

Fold again, tucking corners
behind folds.

7

Flip over. ↩

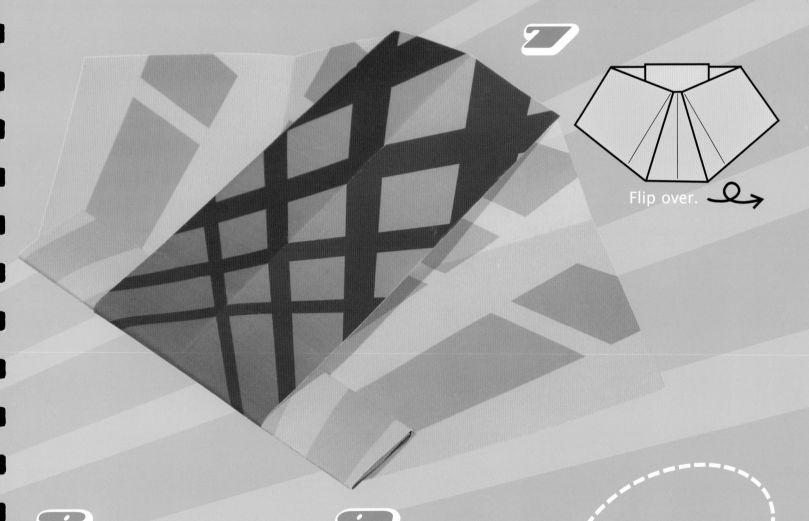

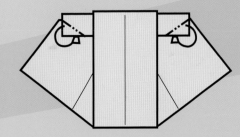

8

Tuck tips under.

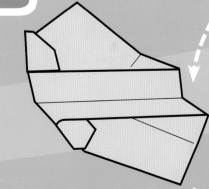

9

Hold from this end.
Place your middle
finger on top and your
first and third finger
underneath. Launch
forward.

Ready for flight!

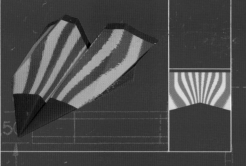

LEVEL TRACK DELTA

Aptly named because when properly adjusted, it flies straight and level to the ground.

1

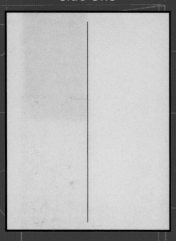

Side One

Fold and unfold to create a vertical middle crease.

2

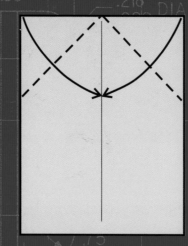

Fold the top two corners in to meet at the middle crease.

3

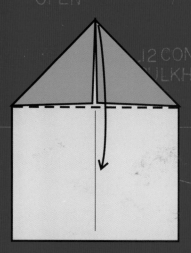

Fold the top point down, creasing just below the flap edges.

4

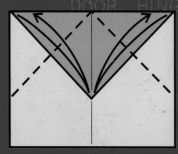

Fold the top corners down to middle crease. Unfold.

5

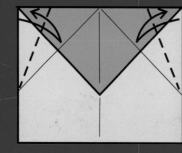

Bring top corners down to creases made in step 4. Unfold.

6

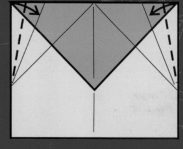

Fold corners in to the creases made in Step 5.

7

Fold left corner down to middle crease just above the point.

8

Repeat Step 7 on the right side.

9

Enlarged view of the middle folds of Step 8.

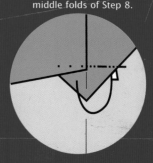

Mountain fold the point just behind the overlapping corner.

Stephen Weiss ©

10

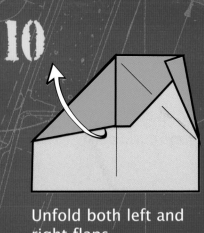

Unfold both left and right flaps.

11

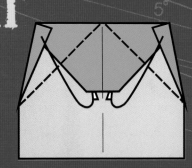

Tuck the flaps underneath the middle layer to lock in place.

12

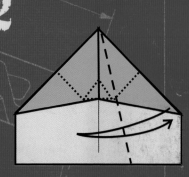

Fold the wing through the corner of the hidden triangle. Unfold. Repeat on the other side.

13

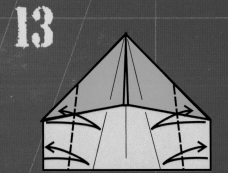

Fold the vertical edge to the wing crease, left and right. Unfold.

14

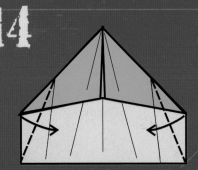

Fold in the wing tips to the reference spots.

15

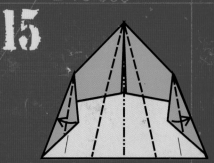

Fold to create both wing tips.

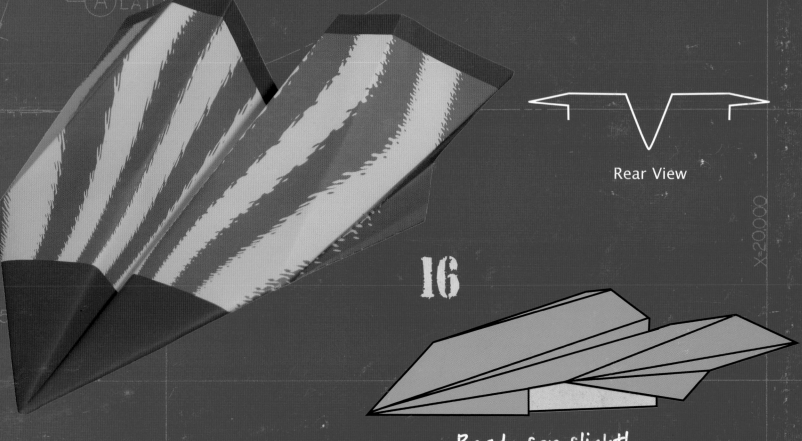

Rear View

16

Ready for flight!

INTERCEPTOR

A sleek flier that travels straight and stays horizontal throughout its flight.

1

Side One

Fold and unfold to create
a vertical middle crease.

2

Fold top left and right
corners in to meet at
the middle crease.

3

Flip over.

4

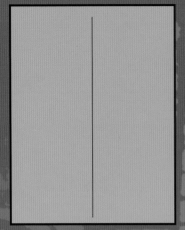

Fold in corners to the
middle crease.

5

Fold in half, dot to dot.

6

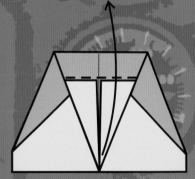

Valley fold the tip up at
the reference line.

7

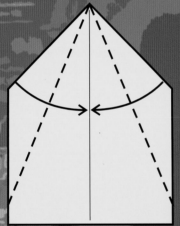

Pull out the layers on each
side, flattening as shown
in diagram 8.

8

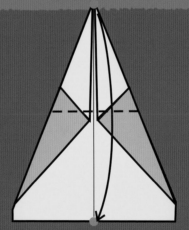

Fold, then unfold, outer
corners. Mountain fold
plane in half.

9

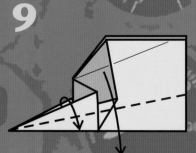

Fold down left wing only.

Stephen Weiss ©

52

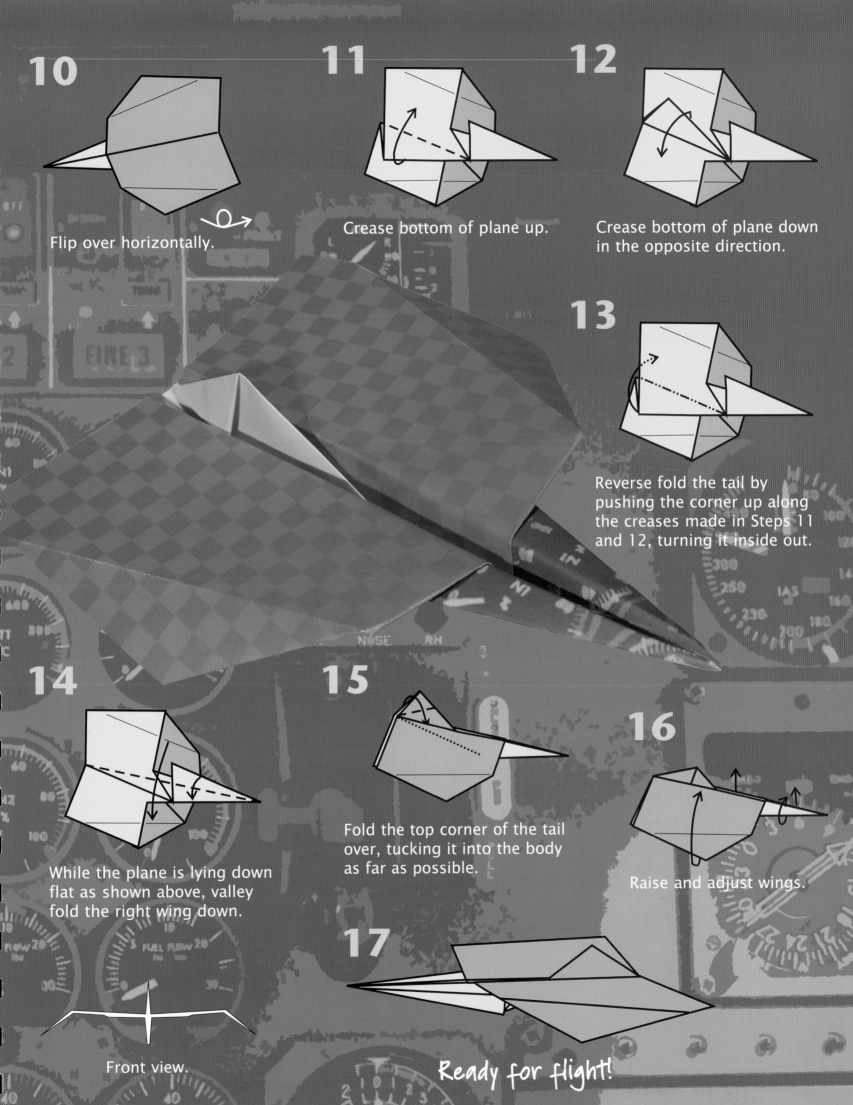

10

Flip over horizontally.

11

Crease bottom of plane up.

12

Crease bottom of plane down in the opposite direction.

13

Reverse fold the tail by pushing the corner up along the creases made in Steps 11 and 12, turning it inside out.

14

While the plane is lying down flat as shown above, valley fold the right wing down.

Front view.

15

Fold the top corner of the tail over, tucking it into the body as far as possible.

16

Raise and adjust wings.

17

Ready for flight!

Flight Test

After folding and creating the 20 different paper planes, test them and see how they fly. Throw them hard or soft, high or low, try them in all sorts of ways and see what tricks get them to fly their best. Fill out the chart below to keep a record of your flight statistics.

Plane Name	Plane Type	Distance Thrown			Time in Flight			Favorite plane on a scale from 1 to 10
		First throw attempt	Second throw attempt	Third throw attempt	First throw attempt	Second throw attempt	Third throw attempt	
Eastern Star								
Straight and Narrow								
Dart Nose								
Fly Paper								
Triumph								
Feather								
Delta Wing								
Albert Ross								
Wisk Wing								
Sky Barge								
Classroom Cruiser								
Hoop-Nosed Scooter								
Canard								
Wind Hawk								
Thunder Bomber								
Bull's-Eye Dart								
Breeze								
Flat Flyer								
Level Track Delta								
Interceptor								